FAIRACRES PUBLICATIONS 228

JOURNEYS INTO THE BIBLE

SISTER EDMÉE SLG

© 2025 SLG Press

First Edition 2025

Fairacres Publications 228

ISBN 978-0-7283-0420-8
Fairacres Publications Series ISSN 0307-1405

SLG Press asserts the right of Sister Edmée SLG to be identified as the author of this work, in accordance with the Copyright Designs and Patents act, 1988.

All rights reserved. No part of this publication may be reproduced, stored in a retrieval system, or transmitted, in any form or by any means, electronic, mechanical, photocopying, recording or otherwise, without the prior permission of the copyright owner.

Translations from the Hebrew Bible are by Sister Edmée. New Testament citations are from the King James Version.

Edited and typeset in Palatino Linotype by Julia Craig-McFeely

SLG Press
Convent of the Incarnation
Fairacres • Oxford
www.slgpress.co.uk

Printed by
Grosvenor Group Ltd, Loughton, Essex

CONTENTS

Acknowledgements	ii
Foreword	iii
A Nun at the Leo Baeck College	1
Kabbalah	7
The Bible, the Jews, and the Spirit of Marcion	16
The Bride and the Beloved	33
On Bringing a Right Spirit to the Old Testament	49
Bibliography	60

Acknowledgements

'A Nun at the Leo Baeck College', first published as 'False Eyelashes at Leo Baeck College', in *Manna: Journal of the Sternberg Centre for Judaism*, 24 (Summer 1989), 8–9.

Extract from 'Kabbalah and the Genius of Gershom Scholem', first published in *Fairacres Chronicle,* 21/3 (Winter 1998), 20–32.

'The Bible, the Jews, and the Spirit of Marcion', first published in *Fairacres Chronicle,* 25/1 (Spring 1992), 15–29.

'The Bride and the Beloved', unpublished talk given at Companions Day, Fairacres Convent, 3 November 2012.

'On Bringing a Right Spirit to the Old Testament', talk given at Fairacres during the Oblates' Week, 28 February 2007, first published in *Fairacres Chronicle,* 40/2 (Winter 2007), 35–45.

Foreword

Between 1972 and 2014 Sr Edmée Kingsmill SLG (1930–2018) published a number of articles in the *Fairacres Chronicle*, the journal of the Sisters of the Love of God at Fairacres. Some of these articles were offshoots of her doctoral work on the Song of Songs,[1] and her excursions into Biblical Hebrew. Essays examining aspects of the Song of Songs that were not part of her dissertation have been gathered together and published as *Divine Love in the Song of Songs* (SLG Press, 2024), while the present volume contains the studies of other texts from the Hebrew Bible and early Christian writers.

Many of her articles were written under the stimulus of a book she had been reading at the time, and started out as reviews but then became an excursion into the theology and philosophy surrounding the subject. Still others were simply an exploration of an idea or fact that had caught her attention and led her down an unexpected byway. Whatever their genesis, the result was an essay crafted from carefully-examined and elegantly-argued ideas and concepts that sweep the reader along in Edmée's wake. She was, at times, unkind to fellow scholars whom she felt had failed to examine their subject thoroughly or without as much rigour as Edmée believed they should have done. Her sometimes caustic asides add spice to her arguments, but also remind the reader of the humanity of the author, and her determined search for answers and for truth in the texts she examined.

This search and determination seem to have been also a defining characteristic of her life as a Religious: David Barton, in his address at her funeral, said that 'she always battled with herself', and that

---

[1] Published as Edmée Kingsmill SLG, *The Song of Songs and the Eros of God: A Study in Biblical Intertextuality* (Oxford University Press, 2009).

battle comes across in her writing, in the ardour with which she puts forth and defends her ideas. She was passionate, too, about her life in the Convent and the wellbeing of her community, the Sisters of the Love of God.

As her mental and physical capacities waned towards the end of her life, no matter what else was lost to her 'she never seemed to lose the sense of being grounded in God', as David Barton commented. Six years after her death, Sister Edmée's articles have been gathered, edited for modern readers (lightly!—she was a formidable editor in her own right, and was editor of SLG Press for many years). They are now published by SLG Press in five modest volumes, ensuring her scholarship and her vocation will reach a wider audience rather than being consigned to the obscurity of back issues of the *Fairacres Chronicle*.

SISTER EDMÉE KINGSMILL SLG

Prayer too Deep for Words, Fairacres Publications 215 (2024).
Divine Love in the Song of Songs, Fairacres Publications 220 (2024).
Bernard & Abelard, Fairacres Publications 222 (2024).
Journeys into the Bible, Fairacres Publications 228 (2025).
Directions, Fairacres Publications 229 (2025).

DIRECTIONS

A Nun at the Leo Baeck College

In 1986, twenty years after my entry into the Anglican contemplative community of the Sisters of the Love of God at Fairacres, Oxford, the course of my monastic life took a radically different turn when I was given permission to devote time to study. This was an exceptional decision, the fruit of a conversation with the then Reverend Mother, Mother Jane, which was subsequently supported by our Warden, Canon Allchin, and the Community Council.

Thus I began, but with much trepidation, for the assumptions which have prevailed in the monastic life have been, in the words of the monk, Thomas Merton, 'that prayer is for saintly women and theological study for practical but, alas, unsaintly men'. But the winds of change are blowing, and if it is an ill one which threatens to bowdlerize the English language, there are other winds blowing quite a lot of good, and I have to acknowledge that I am one of their chief beneficiaries.

The subject which had presented itself within minutes of the prospect being opened up to me was the mystical commentaries on the Song of Songs. I also knew at once that, if he were agreeable (and he was), I would choose Bishop Kallistos Ware for my supervisor, a man deeply learned in the Church Fathers and the Christian mystical tradition—in which no book of the bible has resonated more profoundly than the Song of Songs. It soon became clear to me, however, that in the present climate of thought it would be impossible to treat the great Latin and Greek commentaries convincingly without tackling the Hebrew context and the rabbinical literature—a view which Rabbi Dr Jonathan Magonet, Principal of the Leo Baeck College, firmly endorsed when, by a series of steps at once logical and mysterious, I came to meet him at the Manor House.

Meetings which have important consequences are always memorable. I was at the time learning Latin and expecting to go on to Greek, but I was hoping to avoid having to learn Hebrew as well, and I said so. Dr Magonet, whose handsome appearance and quiet charm immediately disposed me to take everything he said very seriously, took down a *mikraot gedolot* from the shelf and read the opening verse of the Song of Songs: *Shir ha-shirim asher lishelomoh*. 'How do you know', he went on, 'that all those "shshs" haven't some significance?' I groaned and protested my age, but if I wanted to be let off Hebrew I was talking to the wrong man. In any case, I had done enough reading in Jewish sources by the time I met him to appreciate the truth of his contention: that no study of the Song of Songs could get to its heart without some understanding of the language in which it is written. Moreover, were I to become a member of the College—and Dr Magonet offered me a place for a year with the option of dropping out after a term if the aging brain proved not to be up to it (though he put it rather more tactfully)—I would, he explained, have access to many other benefits relevant to my purpose. The hour which I subsequently spent in the library, with Hyam Maccoby effectively proved the point for, as a result of my conversation with him, I acquired two of his finest articles and learnt things in an hour which I could not have learnt independently in a year.

But it was to ask a lot of my Community. The original terms of my study were that I would remain within the enclosure except for taking advantage of the facilities so providentially available in Oxford. But the same capacity for the exceptional decision which had launched me on the path of study now grasped the importance of what was being offered for the subject itself and, with the warm support of our Warden and Bishop Kallistos (who himself takes an active interest in Judaism), Mother Jane gave her permission.

I at once began to learn Hebrew, being fortunate that one of our Sisters, Sister Josephine, had studied it for a theology degree in Oxford and was willing to coach me. Sister Josephine was thus the first of the brethren to learn of my going to the LBC and her reaction augured well: 'I'm glad to hear it', she said, 'I thought when you started this study that you ought to have some proper education!' I am not sure this was quite the view of the rest of the Community, but even those Sisters for whom strict enclosure is important, and who therefore regret any breach of it, have never made me aware of any disapproval, while many Sisters have welcomed this opportunity to learn from the Jews as touching deeply on the vocation of the Community to reconciliation.

Ten months later I joined the College, arriving in time for *Shacharit* on the first day of the new academic year, 12 October 1987. I had asked Dr Magonet during our meeting whether the other students would object to having someone so obviously a nun in their midst and he had assured me they would not, telling me that the first person to take the three-year Diploma Course had been Sister Margaret Shepherd of the Sisters of Zion, 'though', he added, glancing at the long black veil, the full length brown habit and the large cross of Lorraine in the centre of it all, 'I have to admit she was not dressed like that!' But, whatever the other students thought, they certainly accepted this manifestation of another world with every sign of goodwill, and by the time we came to the Feast of Purim the religious habit was sufficiently acceptable for Ron Berry, a fourth-year rabbinical student, to ask me if he might dress up in it for the occasion. Putting Jewish/Christian relations before other considerations, I managed, with the co-operation of our Sister in Charge of the Workroom, to provide him with an outfit which looked identical while not actually employing a consecrated habit. At one moment, when I was winding the girdle round his waist, he burst out laughing and asked, 'Did you ever imagine that one day you'd be dressing up a Jew to look like a nun?' He carried it off splendidly and so I was surprised when he told me later that he had always been frightened of nuns, 'but I'm cured of that now!' he added.

The other half of the story is that, since Ron was now me, the best I could do was to turn up as an 'apocopated *nun*'[1] for which I borrowed

---

[1] Namely, a *nun* (fourteenth letter of the Hebrew alphabet) which has disappeared. But Hebraists will know that the term is not, in fact, applied to *the nun*.

a blonde wig, make-up and false eyelashes plus a pretty blouse and trousers from a model-girl friend, and was unable as a result to get past Dave at the gate. 'Who are you?' he asked ferociously, plainly getting ready to hurl me in front of the only 143 bus to pass the Manor House that morning if I showed the least sign of giving any trouble, but recovering from his surprise when I told him, in time to call after me, 'Don't make an 'abit of it!' During the Purim Spiel a visitor, dressed as an Arab sheikh, declared that 'The security in this place is lousy!' to which I could have added that if it lacked anything in respect of Arab sheikhs it made up for it in respect of blondes wearing false eyelashes!

But long before Purim the preconceptions which inevitably surround nuns had given way to the reality, notably when, for example, Joanne Woolf, a Reconstructionist from the States, ventured to ask how long I had been in my Community. 'Twenty-two years', I told her. 'Ah!' she said gently, 'fresh in at eighteen, I guess?' 'Well, as a matter of fact', I replied, deciding in favour of the truth, 'not-so-fresh in at thirty-five!' 'Oh my! Oh my!' she exclaimed, visibly adjusting to the implications of this disclosure. But even before it no one had felt constrained to modify their language. After all—one sensed the reasoning—if a nun emerges from her cloister into the 'real world' she must **** well take it as she finds it! I came to enjoy the breaks in the Students' Dining-room, but from the first I was especially glad of Miri James, a classmate and the youngest of the rabbinical students, whose unfailing friendliness and good humour often helped me to feel more comfortable than might in the early days have sometimes been the case.

*

Contact with a rather esoteric teaching before my entry into the religious life had alerted me to the dangers of 'identification', but one cannot read Jewish history or study with Jews without becoming identified, and I was soon seeing things from a thoroughly Jewish standpoint. This new perspective, combined with a natural disposition for taking tradition seriously, has been the source of a constant enthusiasm and sense of discovery. Thus, when Rabbi Julia Neuberger—to whose capacity for drawing out the best in her pupils I owe a great deal—set me to work on Leviticus, my sympathy with its place in the tradition enabled me to see that it represents a view of the body which, on the other side of its coin, is profoundly mystical, and that, according to this view, it is the body which is sacred and, consequently, the vehicle of communication with its Creator...

This is very different from the usual view of mysticism, with its Neoplatonic rejection of the body, but it was just such a purely biblical understanding of mysticism that I had hoped for. And, although my previous study of Gershom Scholem had taken me very far in this direction, I think I could not have gained it except in the context of studying rabbinical literature and the tradition as it has developed in Judaism. And here my debt is supremely to the unique quality of Dr Joanna Weinberg's exposition of Mishnah and Midrash which has opened up meanings and connections that would other wise have remained inaccessible to me. Among others from whom I have gained a strong sense of this tradition are Rabbi Jonathan Wittenberg, an especially *simpatico* embodiment of it, and Hyam Maccoby, a brilliant defender of it, with whom I have enjoyed many stimulating conversations. (Of course, there are one or two matters on which I am unable to see quite eye to eye with him but, beyond my wishing him a happy feast day on 25th January—the Conversion of St Paul—we avoid subjects which might adversely affect our blood pressure!)

When, therefore, at the end of my year, I attended the Ordination Service at the West London Synagogue, I was able to appreciate the significance of its predominant theme, explicitly stated in the Opening Prayer: 'God of blessing, we witness today the creation of a new link in the chain of tradition ...' But the 'new links' depend for their formation on something else which was strikingly expressed by Dr Magonet during a Bible class when, after demonstrating the number of ways it is possible to read a text, he said: 'I hope that what we succeed in teaching above all in this College is, quite simply, how to read,'

In January of this year I was permitted to return to the College for a further term and, in response to my plea, our new Mother, Mother Anne, has granted me an extension to cover the summer term as well. After that I look forward to working with Joanna Weinberg on the rabbinical literature relating to the Song, and with Dr Jonathan Webber, a Fellow of the Institute of Social Anthropology in Oxford, on the Hebrew text of the Song itself. I owe Jonathan Webber to the College too, for I came to know him through the Tuesday morning 'Shiur', of which he gave three during my first year. Detecting in him a kindred spirit, I asked him to take me on and have discovered in our sessions a coincidence of approach to the Song I had hardly expected to find any where. That I should have found it here in Oxford is good news for my Community!

Finally, what about the Hebrew language itself, the language of the angels, the holy tongue? Have I found it worth the blood, sweat and tears of trying to learn it? Yes! It is infinitely rewarding, and although I have a long way to go I can already experience something of all that is claimed for it as, for example, in the following passage from Gershom Scholem's *Major Trends in Jewish Mysticism*:

> Language in its purest form, that is, Hebrew, according to the Kabbalists, reflects the fundamental spiritual nature of the world; in other words, it has a mystical value. Speech reaches God because it comes from God.[2]

And so, as I sit at my table overlooking our lovely garden, and read my Hebrew bible during the hour for *Lectio Divina*, it is not inconsistent with the teaching of the Kabbalists if the thought arises, 'Can heaven be much better than this?'

What a lot I owe to that memorable meeting!

---

[2] Gershom Scholem, *Major Trends in Jewish Mysticism,* with a new Foreword by Robert Alter (Schocken, 1995), 17.

Kabbalah

What is the Kabbalah? The term means simply 'tradition', and not until its special use by the disciples of Rabbi Isaac the Blind (c. 1160–1235), an early Kabbalist, did it come to denote a mystical or esoteric tradition. This esoteric tradition is based on a system of symbols which first appeared in Southern France at the end of the twelfth century from whence it spread to Spain in the early years of the thirteenth century. The book *Bahir* was the first to adopt the specific approach and the symbolic structure characteristic of kabbalistic teaching, and it appeared in Provence no earlier than 1150 and probably nearer the end of the century. In any case, by 1200 there were already circles of Kabbalists in Provence, and they belonged, in the words of Isaac the Blind, writing two generations later, 'to the nobles of the land and the propagators of the study of the Torah in the community'.[3] This witness to the impeccably rabbinical character of the first Kabbalists is important because, whatever can be maintained about Gnostic and Neoplatonic influences, it convinces us that the essence of the Kabbalah is authentically Judaic, that is to say, that it is rooted in lifelong study of the scriptures.

The most characteristic symbol of the Kabbalists is the cosmic tree of the worlds, the tree on which are represented the ten *sefirot,* namely, the ten powers or attributes which emanate from the hidden God, the *Ein Sof* (the Infinite), and which represent the aspects of God's being in whose image and likeness we are created. The first *sejrah* is called Crown and also Nothingness because no differentiation exists in it, no 'thingness'. From this *sefirah* all the others flow, the second being Wisdom, the active masculine principle, who impregnates the third *sefirah*, Intelligence or Understanding—the female counterpart of Wisdom. The next seven

---

[3] Gershom Scholem, *Origins of the Kabbalah*, ed. R. J. Zwi Werblowsky, trans. Allan Arkush (Princeton University Press, 1991), 199–200.

sefirah are the result of their union: Love and Judgement, the right and the left arms of God, free-flowing love and strict judgement, grace and limitation, Judgement being also the aspect of evil within the Divine structure.[4] The next *sefirah* is Beauty, also called Compassion, which is the harmonizing principle in the centre of the tree, being in particular the 'son' of Wisdom and Understanding, and his most common name is 'The Holy One, blessed be He'. The next two are Endurance and Majesty which form the right and left legs of the body and are the source of prophecy. The ninth *sefirah*, Foundation, represents the phallus, the procreative power of the universe. He is also called the Righteous One, and Proverbs 10:25 is applied to Him: 'The righteous one is the foundation of the world'. He is the *axis mundi*, the cosmic pillar, through whom the light and power of the preceding *sefirot* are channeled to the last *sejirah*, Kingdom, which is the realm of the Shekhinah. The term Shekhinah was already in use in talmudic literature where it was 'always simply God himself, that is, God insofar as he is present in a particular place or at a particular event'.[5] But medieval Jewish philosophers saw a danger to pure monotheism in the concept as it developed and they all, from Saadya to Maimonides, declared that the Shekhinah was God's free creation, and therefore as a creature, had no part in the divine being or unity of God.[6] One of these philosophers, Yehuda ben Barzilai, writing a generation before the emergence of the Kabbalah, specifically defines this primordial light as the first of all created things, and declares that 'the sages call this great light *Shekhinah*'.[7] What no one had ever said of the

---

[4] Scholem and subsequent commentators write as though the presence of an evil aspect in the being of God was a daring innovation of the Kabbalists and evidence of the introduction of mythology into their system. My own impression is that the biblical foundations of the Kabbalists are being lost sight of here, of such texts, for instance, as 'I form the light and create darkness; I make peace and create evil' (Isaiah 45:7), and 'shall there be evil in the city and the Lord hath not done it?' (Amos 3:6).
[5] Scholem, *Origins of the Kabbalah*, 163.
[6] Christian preachers who complain when it falls to their lot to preach on Trinity Sunday should learn with what difficulty Judaism tries to manage without the concept of a triune God!
[7] Scholem, *Origins of the Kabbalah*, 166–7.

Shekhinah, however, was that it was feminine. This was the innovation of the Kabbalists. They thus introduced into the divine realm a power which they variously describe as the Heavenly Mother, Matron, Queen, the Bride and Wife of the Godhead, Princess, the Divine Daughter, and other similar titles. In his *Major Trends in Jewish Mysticism* Scholem writes:

> The introduction of this idea was one of the most important and lasting innovations of Kabbalism. The fact that it obtained recognition in spite of the obvious difficulty of reconciling it with the conception of the absolute unity of God, and that no other element of Kabbalism won such a degree of popular approval, is proof that it responded to a deep-seated religious need.[8]

This 'deep-seated religious need' had also been felt in Latin Christianity for this was the age of the cult of the Virgin Mary a parallel phenomenon which Scholem does not note. He may have had his reasons for with his wide reading of Christian literature he cannot have been unaware of the numerous and obvious resemblances between the symbolism of the Virgin Mary and the Shekhinah. But if he had seen that perhaps the same forces were at work in both cases—without, moreover, there being any question of cross-influences—he would not, I think, have spent so much time importing Gnosticism into the Kabbalah.

These forces were of a kind, it seems to me, which spanned two millennia and gave the first millennium AD one character, and the second millennium a quite other character (at least in the West, which is where the Kabbalah came to birth). The first millennium was centred on God, which gave it a markedly masculine character. Jewish mysticism in this earlier period—the mysticism of the Chariot (Merkabah) and the writings of the Hekhaloth—manifests this masculine character. It was an active mysticism in which correct calculations and the utmost precision in carrying out those calculations were of the essence. There was much about journeyings and ascent (the most profound metaphor to emerge from this period, 'descenders of the Chariot', notwithstanding). And for the mystics, travelling through the seven heavens to an utterly transcendent God, there were appalling perils

---

[8] Scholem, *Major Trends in Jewish Mysticism*, 229.

and punishments for getting it wrong in any detail. If there is an atmosphere of sublimity at the divine level, there is an atmosphere of scarcely relieved severity at the human level in it all. Scholem concludes the chapter on 'Merkavah mysticism in Major Trends' with a passage which conveys both the sublimity and the severity:

> [The subject of Merkavah mysticism] is never man, be he even a saint. The form of mysticism which it represents takes no particular interest in man as such; its gaze is fixed on God and his aura, the radiant sphere of the Merkavah, to the exclusion of everything else. For the same reason it made no contribution to the development of a new moral ideal of the truly pious Jew. All its originality is on the ecstatical side, while the moral aspect is starved, so to speak, of life ... The ideal to which the Hekhaloth mystic is devoted is that of the visionary who holds the keys to the secrets of the divine realm and who reveals these visions to Israel ...[9]

If we compare this with a passage on the centuries before 1050 in Richard Southern's *Medieval Humanism*, we find a similar atmosphere in Christendom:

> In the main tradition of the early Middle Ages nearly all the order and dignity in the world was closely associated with supernatural power. There was order in symbolism and ritual, and order in worship and sacrament) and both of them were elaborate and impressive. Man's links with the supernatural gave his life a framework of order and dignity; but in the natural order the chaos was almost complete ... Man chiefly knew himself as a vehicle for divine activity ... [He] was an abject being, except when he was clad in symbolic garments, performing symbolic and sacramental acts ...[10]

Southern goes on to say that there was a sharp change of emphasis after about 1050 and that the first signs of the change were to be seen in the monasteries where it 'took the form of a greater concentration on man and on human experience as a means of knowing God'.[11] It was in this changed climate that the cult of the Virgin Mary began to flourish.

---

[9] Scholem, *Major Trends in Jewish Mysticism*, 79.
[10] Richard W. Southern, *Medieval Humanism* (Harper & Row, 1970), 32.
[11] Southern, *Medieval Humanism*, 33.

Mary had, indeed, been important in Christian theology from the beginning, but the controversy in the fifth century, for instance, over her title of *Theotokos*, Mother of God, was concerned with safeguarding the divinity of her Son and was not centred on any symbolism of her own. But now, in the monasteries, exquisite antiphons and hymns were being created in her honour, as also the new Office of Our Lady on Saturday, while in art and architecture she becomes, from about 1130, central. At the popular level, the cult of the Virgin expressed itself in stories of the miraculous, but at another level, the primary level, Mary emerged by the twelfth century as the symbol par excellence of the contemplative life. She thus, in the first centuries of the second millennium, represented humanity in its response to God, a God who now appeared as much immanent as transcendent. The shift of perspective was a radical one, and if it led in due course to a concentration of humanity on itself, that development belongs to later history.

Likewise, in popular devotion and in the celebration of the liturgy, the Shekhinah becomes the mystical Ecclesia of Israel, the bride of the Song of Songs, the 'Virgin Israel' who, at the pilgrim festival of Pentecost (Shavuot), is married to the 'Bridegroom God',[12] the merciful mother of Israel, the symbol of the soul, and much else besides. But, first and foremost, the emergence of the Shekhinah as a feminine principle coincides, as with Mary, with an upsurge of desire for the contemplative life. In neither case does the feminine principle represent Woman: it represents the eros which is at the heart of the contemplation of God. And the shift of perspective is the same:

> Illuminations no longer occur, as in the time of the Merkavah mystics, by way of an ecstatic ascent to the divine Throne. The transmission of celestial mysteries concerning cosmogony and the Merkavah no

---

[12] See, for instance, the chapter 'In the Ritual of the Kabbalists' in Gershom Scholem, *On the Kabbalah and its Symbolism* (Schocken Books, 1975), 137–44. This is Scholem at his most readable and interesting. I recommend it to anyone interested in further reading on the Kabbalah. The other work which must be mentioned is Gershom Scholem, *Kabbalah* (Quadrangle, 1974), a collection based on the major entries written by Scholem for the *Encyclopaedia Judaica* (Meridian, 1978).

longer takes place, either, in the ways indicated in the Hekhaloth literature. The difference is considerable. Instead of rapture and ecstasy we now have meditation, absorption in oneself, and ... inward communion, *debhequth*, with the divine.[13]

'What is really new here', a phrase Scholem uses several times in one form or another in the chapter 'The First Kabbalists in Provence', is this kind of contemplative prayer practised by groups of *perushim* (literally: those who are separated, detached) whose origin is 'connected with the religious enthusiasm that gripped France in the twelfth century, [and found] expression in the Jewish milieu as well as in the surrounding world.' Scholem continues:

> These *perushim* took upon themselves the 'yoke of the Torah' and completely detached their thoughts from the affairs of this world. They did not engage in commerce and sought to attain to purity. The similarities between this phenomenon and Christian monasticism on the one hand and the condition of the *perfecti* or *bonshommes* among the Cathars on the other, are especially striking, despite the clear divergences resulting from the different attitudes of Judaism and Christianity toward celibacy...[14]

All this suggests forces which, as Scholem himself says, 'transcend the boundaries separating Judaism from Christianity'.[15] It is possible that some astrologer could tell us that the period up to the eleventh century was ruled by, for example, Jupiter, and the period following by Venus, but since the planets are themselves only servants of their Creator, like the rest of creation, such a piece of information would indeed be useless. But one finds the notion of a common mood, a phrase which Scholem also uses, more illuminating of the early Kabbalists than his pursuit of Gnostic origins.

Gnostic symbolism may well have abounded. The great cathedrals, dedicated to the Virgin Mary, which were rising in these years—Chartres, Paris, Amiens, Laon, Rouen, Rheims would almost

---

[13] Scholem, *Origins of the Kabbalah*, 247.
[14] Scholem, *Origins of the Kabbalah*, 229–30.
[15] Scholem, *Origins of the Kabbalah*, 238.

certainly yield many a gnostic symbol. Neither can it be doubted that, as with the cathedral builders, there was gnosis among the Kabbalists. Moreover, Scholem's own cavalier use of the term Gnosticism, which he regards as a convenient one covering all manifestations of knowledge of an esoteric and at the same time soteric (redeeming) character, can be justified in relation to Jewish mysticism.[16] But, in so applying the term, it needs to be disassociated from that element in Gnosticism that relates not so much to content as to *disposition,* the disposition which stands apart from the main tradition and, above all, knows better than the main tradition. This aspect of Gnosticism is not evident among these early Kabbalists, and although they did not arise without protest, they not only belonged to the main tradition, but they claimed to *be* the tradition, most significantly in the quarrel with the adherents of Maimonides (the great Jewish Aristotelian philosopher who influenced Aquinas). If the Kabbalists thought they knew better in this quarrel it was not as Gnostics but as contemplatives, in the same way that monks believed that their pondering meditation on the word of God yielded profounder truths than did the discursive intellectualism of the scholastics.

But if the origins of this 'common mood' lie mysteriously in the Godhead, the influence which resonated so profoundly within this mood was clearly discernible—that of Neoplatonism. It is to Neoplatonism, then, that we should look, rather than to Gnosticism, as the fecundating force of the Kabbalah. Scholem, indeed, supplies all the evidence for this view. In addition, he speculates fascinatingly about the possible influence of John Scotus Erigena (the translator of Denys the Areopagite and author of *De divisione naturae* whose works were finally condemned by the Church in 1225) on the Kabbalistic centre at Gerona in Spain.

In the Gerona circle, we meet the greatest of the early Kabbalists, Nahmanides, who entered Christian history through the Disputation of 1263 when his strength of character and courage so impressed the

---

[16] Gershom Scholem, *Jewish Gnosticism, Merkabah Mysticism and Talmudic Tradition* (The Jewish Theological Seminary of America, 1960), 1.

King of Aragon. Nahmanides 'embodied what was best and highest in then Judaism of his time',[17] and in him the intimate connection between *halakhah* (the rabbinical application of the commandments) and Jewish mysticism is perfectly exemplified. His doctrine of 'hidden miracles', as explained by Scholem, is a striking example of his mystical theology (a parallel to which can be found in Augustine's Homily 24 on John):

> This doctrine, repeatedly expounded by Nahmanides as the foundation of the whole Torah, sees the natural law in certain respects as mere appearance behind which is concealed, in reality, a continuum of secret miracles. Hidden miracles are those that give the impression of being nothing more than the effects of the natural course of events, although they are not. In relation to man, the world is not 'nature' at all but a perpetually renewed miracle … The blessedness of man depends upon his acceptance of this doctrine.[18]

Origins of the Kabbalah takes the subject to the 1250s or thereabouts when 'the Kabbalah already appears in full flower and in all its vigour'.[19] From that period on the Kabbalists began to compose major works, and the most major of these was the *Zahar*, about which Scholem writes in *Major Trends in Jewish Mysticism*:

> In the years immediately following 1275 … a book was written somewhere in the heart of Castile which was destined to overshadow all other documents of Kabbalist literature by the success and the fame it achieved and the influence it gradually exerted; this was the *Sefer ha-Zohar*, or 'Book of Splendour'. Its place in the history of Kabbalism can be gauged from the fact that alone among the whole of post-Talmudic rabbinical literature it became a canonical text which, for a period of several centuries, actually ranked with the Bible and the Talmud.[20]

It could be said that with the *Zohar* there was already some loss of the original purity, a movement from the contemplative to the affective

---

[17] Scholem, *Origins of the Kabbalah*, 389.
[18] Scholem, *Origins of the Kabbalah*, 453.
[19] Scholem, *Origins of the Kabbalah*, 475.
[20] Scholem, *Major Trends in Jewish Mysticism*, 157.

level. But it was precisely this 'loss' which made it accessible to the Jewish people as a whole, for whom it became 'the expression of all that was profoundest and most deeply hidden in the innermost recesses of the Jewish soul'.[21] The Enlightenment put an end to its influence for European Jewry and, as we saw at the beginning of this article, the Kabbalah then fell prey to charlatans and worse—with whom it is still to be found. Whether its misuse by practitioners of black magic and cult groups indicates an inherent flaw is a question which may reasonably be asked. I believe, rather, that the symbolism of the Cosmic Tree expresses mysteries so sacred that, like the Blessed Sacrament, it needs to be kept under lock and key except when it is in the hands of its accredited ministers.

---

[21] Scholem, *Major Trends in Jewish Mysticism*, 157.

The Bible, the Jews, and the Spirit of Marcion

We have recently read in refectory at our midday meal *A Rabbi's Bible* by Jonathan Magonet, a book we have all enjoyed immensely.[22] Magonet is a sparkling writer whom one would like to see chained to his desk and prevented from doing any work other than writing such books. But he is too distinguished a figure, too important as an ambassador for British Jewry, to be allowed to live for long in the privacy of the study.

Rabbi Dr Jonathan Magonet is Principal of Leo Baeck College, the Reform/Liberal seminary for the training of the rabbinate and study of Judaism, where I spent five terms in 1988–9, and where I was privileged to study the Bible in classes with Dr Magonet. I am, therefore, familiar with the approach of *A Rabbi's Bible*, in particular with the approach set out in the chapter 'Learning How to Read', of which I recall Dr Magonet saying, after demonstrating the number of ways it is possible to read (or misread) a text, 'I hope that what we succeed in teaching above all in this College is, quite simply, how to read.'

There is, of course, much else that is taught at Leo Baeck (training for the rabbinate takes five years), and some of it is beautifully described in *A Rabbi's Bible*, especially in the chapter 'Open Rebuke and Hidden Love' where the contents of one page of the Rabbinic Bible, with its Targums[23] in Aramaic and commentaries in a Hebrew script quite different to the biblical, takes more than two pages to describe.[24] Thus, as Magonet tells us, the Pentateuch alone takes up two volumes,

---

[22] Jonathan Magonet, *A Rabbi's Bible* (SCM Press, 1991).
[23] A Targum is the word used of the translation of a biblical book into the vernacular, namely, into Aramaic.
[24] Magonet, *A Rabbi's Bible*, 48–51.

each the size of a telephone directory. This chapter leads on logically to one on interpretation, 'How a Donkey Reads the Bible', while the next, 'My Part in the Fall of King David', is a witty account of the author's experience of being an adviser during the filming of a biblical epic which provoked some of us to near helpless laughter. There is a particularly fine last chapter and we all felt a sense of regret when we came to the end of the book. I cannot precisely pin-point the charm of *A Rabbi's Bible,* but great charm there is as the author engages with and illumines different aspects of the Bible, presenting with much profundity and psychological acuity the different responses it arouses in the reader.

This chapter, however, is not intended as a review of *A Rabbi's Bible* but rather to make use of it as a stepping-stone to the discussion of certain problems in regard to the Bible which have emerged among Christians in recent years following a fundamental change of attitude to the Jews. Reflection on the mystery of the Holocaust, a reflection which increases and deepens with time, has had, and will continue to have, an impact on Christian theology and the way it expresses itself, far greater than most of us yet realize. But, inevitably, in our efforts to get it right we are going to get it wrong, and some of this getting it wrong needs to be noticed—or so it seems to me. But, before looking at some examples, let us look at a passage in *A Rabbi's Bible* which also gets it wrong, and in so doing provides a first stepping-stone to our subject.

I

In a discussion of the interpretation by Rashi, the greatest of all Jewish commentators (1040–1105), of Jacob pretending to be Esau (Gen. 27:18–24), Magonet offers an explanation for Rashi's 'highly dubious way of justifying Jacob's unjustifiable behaviour' by suggesting that Rashi was under pressure from the Christians: 'Jacob symbolized Israel, so every detail of his behaviour would be open to scrutiny as a way of attacking the community'.[25] But, on the contrary, the medieval

---

[25] Magonet, *A Rabbi's Bible*, 20.

Christian exegesis of this story in the Latin West (Rashi was a native of Troyes) was derived from Augustine who saw Jacob as a type of Christ, taking upon himself the sins of humanity—the skins of the goats—and extracting from his father the blessing of the first-born in order that he might redeem the failure of the firstborn, the one who had despised his birthright. So Rashi could have been responding to this high view of Jacob, but he could equally have been trying to keep in line with his own tradition in which three of the Targums on Genesis 28:12 picture the angels who accompany Jacob ascending to heaven to bring other angels down to 'see the pious man whose features are fixed on the throne of glory ...',[26] which suggests that the Rabbis also understood Jacob's deception as 'no lie but a mystery', in the words of St Augustine.[27]

What is unexpected is Magonet's assumption concerning the Bible itself. He has slipped into thinking of it as belonging solely to the Jews. And no wonder! Let us see the kind of encouragement which such a view is receiving from Christians themselves.

A typical example of the trend comes from an Oxford University sermon called 'Jews and Christians' given by a former Archbishop of Canterbury. In giving reasons 'why an attitude of "confuting" the Jews ... is inappropriate today', Donald Coggan claimed that the Church owes an immense debt to Judaism, a debt such as to be impossible of repayment, for without the Jewish people we should never have had what we Christians call the Old Testament.[28] He continues:

---

[26] See Christopher Rowland, 'John 1.51, Jewish Apocalyptic and Targumic Tradition', *New Testament Studies*, 30 (1984), 498–507, in which the four Targumim on Gen. 28:12 are conveniently set out. I am indebted to Professor Rowland for drawing my attention to this article which is a particularly fine example of how Jewish texts can illumine Christian texts.

[27] *The Moral Treatises*: 'To Consentius: Against Lying' (from the *Retractions*, Book II, chap. 60), trans. H. Browne, in *Nicene and Post-Nicene Fathers*, First Series, vol. 3, ed. Philip Schaff (Christian Literature Publishing Co., 1887), 481–500.

[28] Donald Coggan, 'Jews and Christians', *Theology*, 93 (July 1990), 262.

> If Greece has introduced us to the ways of philosophy and to the rigours of thought; if Rome has given us the basics of law and government, it is to *Israel* that we look for an introduction to a God who is at once a God of justice and compassion ... How immense is the debt which the Christian owes to the Jew! Should we not, in an attitude of gratitude, learn from, rather than seek to 'confute' the Jew?[29]

This may *sound* splendid but, firstly, the biblical books are not the product of Judaism and therefore to say the Church owes an immense debt to Judaism is historically inaccurate. The *Encyclopaedia Judaica* makes it clear that to refer to the biblical religion as 'Judaism' is anachronistic, 'both because there were no Jews ... in the formative period of the Bible, and because there are distinctive features which mark off later Judaism from the earlier forms, ideas and worship'.[30]

Secondly, to say that without the Jewish people we should never have had the Old Testament is not only anachronistic but has lost sight of a right Christian understanding: that we, no less than the Jews, *are* the Israelites of the biblical books. It is therefore *as Israel* that we enjoy whatever comes to us from Greece and Rome, and if we now blush to call ourselves *verus Israel*, 'the true Israel', Israelites nevertheless, whether true or false, we are and must remain.

Such thinking as we find in the passage from Dr Coggan's sermon is, however unintentionally, more likely to lead to the rejection of the Old Testament and the spirit of Marcion than to gratitude. The same may also be feared concerning the chapter on Jews in Harvey Cox's *Many Mansions*,[31] in which Cox's good intentions, like those of Dr Coggan, lead him to take the same line. Other examples touch the subject only in passing but often in a manner symptomatic of the confusion which increased awareness of Judaism without increased knowledge is generating in regard to the Bible. In another of our refectory reading books, *A Step Too Far* by Robin Green, the author,

---

[29] Coggan, 'Jews and Christians', 262–3.
[30] Louis Jacobs, 'Judaism', *Encyclopaedia Judaica*, vol. 11 (Thomson Gale, 2007), 511–20, here 512.
[31] Harvey Cox, *Many Mansions: A Christian's Encounter with Other Faiths* (Collins, 1988), 9–10.

referring to the struggles recorded in Acts 15 and Galatians 2, writes: 'At first glance the conflict, like many other human confrontations, seems to be about comparatively minor matters: circumcision and the eating of particular animals',[32] after which one did not expect to hear a reference to 'Jewish traditions'—which, however, turned out to be the book of Exodus. Neither was 'Jewish traditions' an attempt to avoid 'Old Testament' for this title is used on the very next page. But some writers are replacing 'Old Testament' with 'Judaism' when quoting biblical books. Which brings us to Jewish objections to the title 'Old Testament'.

II

Jonathan Magonet discusses the problem, even among Jews, of what to call the 'library of books known as the Bible' and, regarding the Christian title, he tells us: 'For Jews to hear that their "Testament" is "Old" and therefore in some way superseded by the "New" is unacceptable'.[33] Yes, that Christians are becoming sensitive about giving offence to the Jews on this point is one of the principal factors in our increasing use of anachronistic and, as I hope to show, Marcionite, terminology. But if we dropped 'Old Testament' what else could we call it?

Before we consider alternatives, I have to say that if this title still worked for Christians I believe we would have to keep it. But Jewish objections (which, I have the impression, are quite modern) reflect a state of mind among Christians, especially 'liberal' Christians, which renders the title 'Old Testament' an insuperable barrier to its understanding. The theory of evolution, with concomitant notions of 'progress', has created a network of assumptions which regards anything 'old' as obsolescent, namely, as the dictionary defines that word, going out of use or out of fashion. The opposite assumptions prevailed when the title 'Old Testament' was given. In those early centuries of Christianity, when both Jews and Christians were influenced by

---

[32] Robin Green, *A Step too Far* (Darton, Longman & Todd, 1990), 55.
[33] Magonet, *A Rabbi's Bible*, 9–10.

Hellenistic ideas, it was a question of the older the better. (An example is the defence of the antiquity of the Jews by Josephus in his work *Against Apion*, and Origen's warm approval of this defence and his use of it to confute Celsus.[34]) But the belief that the further back one goes the nearer one will be to the source of wisdom is simply no longer with us, and for that reason I join those who favour a new title for the Old Testament. What are the alternatives?

There are two which have already come into use, the 'Jewish Scriptures' and the 'Hebrew Bible'. The first of these, the 'Jewish Scriptures', is being used by an increasing number of Christian scholars who should know better, one example being Frances Young who, in her book, *The Art of Performance*, almost invariably uses this designation.[35] The *Art of Performance* is so good, especially the chapter 'Bible and Spirituality', and what Professor Young is doing in it (which is to help those who have 'done' theology to read the tradition again) is so important that I would have commended it without reservation but for the way it issues a Decree Absolute on the divorce between the two testaments. For instance, one of the chapters is entitled 'Jewish Texts and Christian Meanings', and most of the chapter itself is similarly loaded in the same misleading direction. Professor Young must know that 'Jewish texts', properly so called, begin with the Mishnah and that no serious Jewish scholar would refer to the biblical books as 'Jewish texts' (Magonet nowhere does); why then should a Christian—except to make the point that they belong by right to the Jewish people alone? But that is the point she does make: 'With our changed perspectives, we would do well to feel embarrassed about the way our forebears, in such a high-handed and insensitive way, commandeered the sacred books that really belong to the on-going Jewish community'.[36]

---

[34] See, for instance, Louis H. Feldman, *Jew and Gentile in the Ancient World: Attitudes and Interactions from Alexander to Justinian* (Princeton University Press, 1993), 219 and 321.
[35] Frances Young, *The Art of Performance: Toward a Theology of Holy Scripture* (Darton, Longman and Todd, 1990).
[36] Young, *The Art of Performance*, 63.

I first met this viewpoint some years ago in a German Lutheran who criticized our monastic office for being based on 'their'–namely, the Jews'–psalms, a view which, it soon became clear, concealed a suppressed anti-Semitism. But even if this view is not based in anti-Semitism it is, I believe, liable to lead to it. For if Christians come to accept that they have no right to or, at best, are borrowing the very scriptures which Jesus 'beginning at Moses and all the prophets ... expounded to them in all the scriptures concerning himself' so that their hearts burned within them (cf. Luke 24:27 and 32), how shall our hearts burn within us when the Holy Spirit likewise opens those same scriptures to us? And hearts that do not burn, grow cold, as they did in Germany in the wake of Wellhausen, whose critical work on the Old Testament effectively divorced it from the New and generated an increasing anti-Semitism both in himself and in his followers, ultimately contributing to an ethos in which Christian theologians impotently continued their work while Jews were being eliminated from their midst.

Perhaps a connection between that shameful fact and the desire to make reparation to the Jews by the heirs of German criticism has long ago been noted. In any case, it is in the liberal scholarly establishment where the most influential reparation is taking place, and Frances Young is right to be in the spirit of it. But there can be no reparation at the expense of truth or it will rebound and produce consequences opposite to those intended. Was it 'high-handed' of those Jews to hold on to their own scriptures after believing that one from among them had revealed their true meaning? There would be high-handedness and insensitivity down the centuries, God knows, once Christianity became established, but it matters that we do not slanderously transfer later attitudes to the first Jewish followers of Jesus. No, at the parting of the ways each side in the struggle retained the scriptures which were their own, adjusting them, as we shall see when we consider the title 'Hebrew Bible', to harmonize with their convictions, and thus the scriptures became the Jewish scriptures for the Jews and the Christian scriptures for the Christians. The title 'Jewish Scriptures' should not, therefore, be appropriated by Christians since it falsely bridges a division: one that cannot be bridged by goodwill alone.

III

At first sight the 'Hebrew Bible' seems the better candidate to replace 'Old Testament' since Hebrew is the language in which the majority of its books were written. But this title cannot be considered apart from the Jewish canon on the one hand and the Christian canon on the other, a subject on which Magonet makes a polemical point, once again providing a stepping-stone—though in this case 'springboard' would be a better description. 'There is', he writes, 'a "built-in" ordering of the biblical books that makes for a major difference in perception between Jews and Christians', and he goes on to compare the Hebrew order with that in the King James version which inserts into the Hebrew division of 'Former Prophets'.

> the book of Ruth (following Judges), Ezra, Nehemiah and I and II Chronicles. That is to say, the ordering seems to be based on seeing these volumes as 'historical' ... Since they are identical books, does the change of sequence matter?[37]

Magonet goes on to study the rise to power of Abimelech in Judges 9, which he compares with the rise to power of a Hitler, and his conclusion—that 'the answer of the Hebrew Bible in terms of the actual ordering of the books is that they are to be read as "prophecy"'[38]—is extremely important. But it was the comparison with the King James version which provided the springboard and plunged me into the canon question, and the view of it I have come up with is rather different, though Magonet's point remains, namely, that the Bible *should* be read as prophecy (in the sense of challenging 'those who are at ease in Zion' (Amos 6:1)) and not as history.

The King James version, apart from following the mistaken scholarship of the Reformers in separating some books as 'apocryphal', did not, of course, follow a line of its own in the ordering of books but followed the Vulgate which in turn took its order from the Septuagint, the translation into Greek of the Hebrew Bible in the third to second

---

[37] Magonet, *A Rabbi's Bible*, 68–9.
[38] Magonet, *A Rabbi's Bible*, 72.

century BC. The question then arises: Who did the altering? That is to say, does the Septuagint represent the original order, departed from by the Jews in the Hebrew Bible as part of their redefinition of Judaism against the Christians, or was the order of books in the Septuagint altered by Christians after the Jews, realizing the support some of its readings were giving to Christian interpretations, had abandoned it to Christian use altogether?

This is a highly complex question and should not be ventured into before reading John Barton's admirable and judicious presentation of the evidence in the first two chapters of his *Oracles of God*.[39] Nevertheless, because Professor Barton entertains notions of 'accident', I take for the present purpose two scholars who, writing about their own traditions, allege conscious intention in the different emphases of the two canons. The first is from the article 'Allegorical Interpretation' by Andrew Louth:

> From evident prophecies of the Messiah, Christians ... ultimately regarded the whole of the scriptures (viz. the 'Old Testament') as prophetic—prophetic of Jesus (this is reflected in the way Christians began to reorganize the 'Old Testament' so that it led up to, and culminated in the prophetic books). Such a 'prophetic interpretation of the OT is a form of allegory as it treats the whole Bible as speaking one thing (viz. about the religious experience of Israel) and signifying something other than what is said (viz. the fulfilment of all in Jesus).[40]

The second example comes from the article in the *Jewish Encyclopedia* of 1902 on Rabbi Akiba (c. AD 50–c. 132), by the immensely learned Louis Ginzberg, in which he states: 'Akiba was the one who definitely fixed the canon of the Old Testament books.' (Note the use of 'Old Testament' by a Jewish scholar writing for Jews.[41]) And:

---

[39] John Barton, *Oracles of God: Perceptions of Ancient Prophecy in Israel after the Exile* (Darton, Longman & Todd, 1986).

[40] Andrew Louth, 'Allegorical Interpretation', in *A Dictionary of Biblical Interpretation*, ed. R. J. Coggins and J. L. Houlden (SCM Press, 1990), 12–14, here 12.

[41] Louis Ginzberg, 'Akiba Ben Joseph', *The Jewish Encyclopedia*, vol. i: Aach–Apocalyptic Literature (Funk and Wagnalls Company, 1907), 304–10, here 305.

> To the same motive underlying his [Akiba's] antagonism to the Apocrypha, namely the desire to disarm Christians—especially Jewish Christians—who drew their 'proofs' from the Apocrypha, must also be attributed his wish to emancipate the Jews of the Dispersion from the domination of the Septuagint, the errors and inaccuracies in which frequently distorted the true meaning of scripture, and were even used as arguments against the Jews by the Christians.[42]

So Aquila, the Bible translator, under Akiba's guidance, gave the Greek-speaking Jews a rabbinical Bible—thus, Ginzberg tells us, in another part of the article, 'Judaizing the Bible, as it were, in opposition to the Christians'.[43] The chief element in this 'Judaizing' was a profound emphasis on Torah:

> As the fundamental principle of his system, Akiba enunciates his conviction that the mode of expression used by the Torah is quite different from that of every other book.[44]

The interest of both these examples lies not in concrete evidence, which is wanting for both of them, but in their correspondence with results—however they came about. That is to say, a canon which culminates with Malachi (the Christian order) is clearly reflecting a different understanding to that of a canon which culminates with I and II Chronicles (the Hebrew order). The different orders of books represent distinct theologies, and if we call our 'Old Testament' the 'Hebrew Bible' we are implying not only a common scripture but a common tradition of use and interpretation.

This last point was made by Krister Stendahl during a lecture at Wolfson College, Oxford on 3 May 1990. Professor Stendahl, much of whose academic work is devoted to the relationship of Jews and Christians, went on to wonder whether 'First and Second Testament' might be explored for Christian use. This could be the answer, though the danger of identifying the Jews with the 'First' Testament and the

---

[42] Ginzberg, 'Akiba Ben Joseph', 306.
[43] Ginzberg, 'Akiba Ben Joseph', 306.
[44] Ginzberg, 'Akiba Ben Joseph', 307.

Christians with the 'Second' would remain. My own thought is that we might call the two parts in Christian Bibles Part I and Part II which, although derisorily simple, has the advantage of not implying supersession or any contrast between the God of the Old Testament and the God of the New, against which Magonet protests:

> There is a particularly crude form of religious one-upmanship that tries to put down the image of God in the Old Testament as a God of anger and general nastiness at the expense of the God of the New Testament who is the God of love. The theory is patently absurd, as even the most casual reading of both Testaments will indicate.[45]

Yes, indeed. What Magonet is describing is the spirit of Marcion which has re-emerged in our day, and not only among those who practise religious one-upmanship. Who was Marcion?

IV

Marcion lived in the second century but he was in all respects except one (he ruled out sex altogether, even within marriage) a very 'modern' man whose system contained elements from which the Church could have benefited had they not been combined with others which were lethal to Christianity. For instance, he favoured democracy in church management, was against a rigid distinction between clergy and laity, and permitted women to hold office on the Pauline principle that 'in Christ there is neither male nor female', though he retained the Pauline prohibition against women speaking in church.

His extraordinary success was not based on extraordinary claims. He did not, as Edwin Blackman writes,[46] come forward as a prophet with 'the word of the Lord came unto me saying', neither did he appeal to any secret tradition. So he was not a Gnostic, but what made him dangerous was that, like the Gnostics, he maintained that Christianity began with Christ. He therefore distinguished the God of the Jews and the God of the Christians, the God of the Jews being the

---

[45] Magonet, *A Rabbi's Bible*, 120.
[46] Edwin C. Blackman, *Marcion and his Influence* (SPCK, 1948), 8. The brief sketch of Marcion given here depends largely on this book.

Creator God, just but severe and cruel, while the God of the Christians was the higher God, the God of love, unknown except as he was revealed in Christ. Judgement was the prerogative of the Creator God; redemption the free gift of the God of love. The revelation in Christ was intended to replace not to fulfil the scriptures, and the one had no connection with the other. Those Christian writings which did not support this view he rejected, which left him with a shortened version of Luke and ten of the Pauline epistles. Against all the rest he maintained his conviction that they had been falsified by Judaizers.

Marcion's contrast between Law and Gospel was vigorously and successfully controverted by Tertullian, Irenaeus and others, but the element of discontinuity in the New Testament itself ensures that Marcionism will re-emerge when conditions favour a humanistic over a biblical understanding of scripture. A major contribution to the spirit of Marcion was made by the Swedish Lutheran theologian Anders Nygren in his book *Agape and Eros,* the first part of which was translated into English in 1932. It met with extraordinary success, and by the time both parts were published in one volume had become recommended reading in our theological colleges.[47] If few actually read it, its success may be measured by the fact that everyone nevertheless came to be influenced by it.[48]

Nygren, indeed, shows Marcion to have been mistaken, but on the way to this conclusion he reinforces the νόμος *(nómos)*—Law—and ἀγάπη *(agápē)*—Love—contrast to such effect as wonderfully to serve the cause of Marcion, especially in his attack on Tertullian. Nygren's book has been profoundly damaging with its combination of learning and compelling air of verisimilitude, above all in its treatment of the nomos/agape motif which the reader is inevitably deceived into thinking a minor matter in comparison with the main agape/eros motif and therefore less worthy of resistance. But the contrast between nomos and agape is false and far-reachingly dangerous, for agape is at the heart of nomos. Or, rather, because the distinction between agape and eros is

---

[47] Anders Nygren, *Agape and Eros*, trans. Philip S. Watson (SPCK, 1953).
[48] See below, p. 53.

not applicable here, the English word 'love', which includes them both, is better, so that we may say: 'Love' is the heart of 'Law'. And this, if only we understood it, is what the Song of Songs is all about. Hence the rabbinical saying, attributed to Rabbi Akiba: 'Had the Torah not been given, the Song of Songs would have sufficed to guide the world.'[49]

While I was pondering the spirit of Marcion a book came into my hands, *The Enigma of Evil* by John Wenham,[50] which cannot fail to dispel any such spirit in its readers, for which reason I warmly commend it–all the more so because it is easy to read, being beautifully and simply written.

Wenham takes the Bible whole. There is no difference in the two parts, he maintains, and no problems in the Old Testament which are not also to be found in the New. In a chapter called 'Cursings' he shows that the 'imprecatory' psalms can be computed as occurring by allusion or quotation more than twice as often in the New Testament as any of the others. ;Had they been alien to the spirit of the New Testament', he writes, 'one might have expected to have found them tacitly shunned by its writers'.[51]

Wenham is concerned to show that the liberalization of the Bible makes it less relevant to the suffering of the world, not more, and he convincingly brings together the God of 'infinite wrath and infinite love', showing us that we cannot have one without the other. Most importantly, he challenges the sentimental picture of Jesus which Christians tend to maintain in the face of the Gospel accounts. But it is all done with a thoughtfulness and even tenderness which is sometimes deeply moving.

A weakness, although in context I am not sure it is not a strength, is that the interpretative framework of the author excludes

---

[49] See *Agadath Shir Hashirim, Edited from a Parma Manuscript. Annotated and Illustrated with Parallel Passages from Numerous MSS. and Early Prints, with a Postscript on the History of the Work*, ed. Solomon Schechter (Deighton Bell & Co., 1896), 5, my translation.
[50] John Wenham, *The Enigma of Evil: Can We Believe in the Goodness of God?* (Inter-Varsity Press, 1985).
[51] Wenham, *The Enigma of Evil*, 157.

any understanding other than a strictly literal one. Allegory he regards as next to lunacy, and there must be no evasion of what has been revealed, which means that all is to be taken at the level of the letter. But let us look briefly at the notorious conclusion to Psalm 137, which crops up in the book more than any of the other Psalms, and see whether a metaphorical interpretation is not an enrichment rather than an evasion of its meaning:

> O daughter of Babylon ...
> Blessed be the one who takes your little ones and dashes them
> against the rock! (Ps. 137:8–9)

I examine this more fully below (p. 56), but to summarize my more detailed examination there, the word for 'little ones' here is *olel*, literally 'sucklings', a rare word usually occurring in passages where word play and metaphor are evident and in contexts of threats, disaster and death. The word for 'rock', *sela*, is often a metaphor for 'truth' and, more explicitly, for God, as in 2 Samuel 22:2, ('The Lord is my rock and my fortress'), and Psalms 18:2, 31:3, 42:9 and 71:3. An interpretation of what the psalmist intends to convey could therefore be: 'Happy is the one who takes the lies suckled by power (namely, Babylon), and dashes them against the truth, the rock, the God of Israel.'

But if I part company with Wenham on interpretation I am enthusiastically with him in the attempt to look the Bible unflinchingly in the eye. It is the failure to do so which, I have come to believe, is the ground of much Christian anti-Semitism. The difficulties of the Old Testament have increased incalculably with the rise of humanism (for Jews even more than for Christians since, as we have seen, Christians can take refuge in a Marcionite form of Christianity), but the difficulty of facing Jesus was there from the beginning. Thus, throughout the centuries, when not only a Christian's career but his very life often depended on the profession of orthodox beliefs, this difficulty has been projected on to the 'unbelieving Jews'. But, more than orthodox beliefs, and much more subtle, is the difficulty that as I read the Gospel accounts I come up against a man I have to admit to myself I would not, in all probability, have understood at the time (if, indeed, I understand him now). I might even have disliked him and in the end found him intolerable. Psychologically I either face up to the fact that the truth of Jesus would have been beyond my capacity to bear without the benefit of hindsight, or I repress as I read and adopt the kind of sentimental picture of Jesus that Wenham endeavours to dispel. But in this latter case the unacknowledged fears concerning my spiritual blindness must find an object. Hence the kind of anti-Jewish polemic which is now infinitely distressing to read.

In recent times, however, the projection has tended to take the opposite form of identifying with the Jewish position and is to be found in much biblical scholarship–where it is thought to provide 'objectivity'. But, however suspect some of this identification might appear, it is vastly to be preferred to its opposite. Which brings me to my final section and a resource book of biblical scholarship which, after an hour or two's browsing, gave me a strong sense of where we are getting it right in regard to Judaism and the Jews.

V

The book is *A Dictionary of Biblical Interpretation* (from which I have already quoted above) and is, as the blurb rightly claims, 'an essential handbook and reference work for all who are interested in serious study of the Bible'.[52] In their admirable Preface the editors state: 'one of our concerns has been to avoid Christian triumphalism and give due weight to Jewish interpretation'. Given the 'school' the *Dictionary* represents there would have been no effort involved in avoiding Christian triumphalism but the 'due weight to Jewish interpretation' has assured a character to the collection which makes it apt for that work of reparation which, as we saw, is owed to the Jews by the heirs of German criticism.

And it is not only a matter of reparation. We see from the *Dictionary*, in addition to the Jewish contributors, that there is now a generation of Christian scholars who have become competent in the

---

[52] *A Dictionary of Biblical Interpretation*, ed. R. J. Coggins and J. L. Houlden (SCM Press, 1990). A paperback edition was issued in 1992.

complex fields of Rabbinics, Apocalyptic and early Jewish mysticism, and whose work in these areas is doing far more than providing an interesting backdrop to Christian theology. One begins to see, indeed, that, properly understood, early Jewish writings can illumine Christian texts in a way which casts fresh light or restores understanding we have lost.

There are disappointments in the *Dictionary* articles, of course, one being 'Rabbi, Rabbinism' by Philip Alexander who writes on this subject as a Protestant might write on Roman Catholic sacerdotalism down the ages. Consequently, justice is not done to the rise of the rabbinical genius after the destruction of the Second Temple in AD 70 and the astonishing recovery of Judaism under such great men as Rabbi Akiba—who is not even mentioned. The 'demythologizing' influence of the American Jewish scholar Jacob Neusner (1932–2016), which is bedevilling the study of Rabbinics at the time of writing, is omnipresent.[53] Neusner has to be read because with his staggering prolificity he is often the only modern writer to have covered a subject in Rabbinics the student needs to study. But that he does not understand in any profound way what he writes about is worryingly evident and one wonders whether Jewish tradition will survive him as well as Christian theology has survived his model, Rudolf Bultmann.

But, having entered that caveat, the *Dictionary* is enriched by a host of excellent articles which do indeed 'give due weight to Jewish interpretation'—including Alexander's on 'Midrash', once one has got past his gross misapplication of the term to include the Septuagint and the New Testament. Among those contributors on overlapping themes one should mention especially Robert M'Cheyne's (on Jewish Christianity) and Sebastian Brock (on Syriac tradition) because they have both long been leading the way in a style of Christian/Jewish scholarship which, it is now easy to see, is prophetic of future developments. And while there is much else (bad, it has to be said, as well as good) in the *Dictionary of Biblical Interpretation* it is, I believe, its bias toward Jewish tradition which will take it into the twenty-first century.

---

[53] In 2016 Neusner was named as one of the most published authors in history, having written or edited more than 900 books.

All four Gospels tell us that Pilate put a superscription on the Cross of Jesus which read 'King of the Jews', but John, who for such details is rightly called 'the theologian', adds that it was written in Hebrew, Greek and Latin. Looking back on two thousand years of Christian interpretation we see that the Greek and the Latin seams have been exhaustively mined. Now, it would appear, it is the turn of the Hebrew.

The Bride and the Beloved[*]

I

THE BRIDE

The Bride in the Song of Songs, that is to say, the figure who most often speaks in the first person, and is most often addressed directly by the messianic figure, called the beloved, is not a woman but a series of metaphors. Among these she represents the land of Israel, the people of Israel, the city of Jerusalem, the Torah, both written and oral. But all these are subsumed under the one role: she is the Temple. The more closely one looks at the curious descriptions of her the more it can be seen that she is what, in Christian usage, would come to be called 'the Bride of Christ', that is, the Church. It has taken me many years of close reading to become clear about this but, once seen, a great deal previously incomprehensible, begins to make sense. But here I am going to look at the Bride as representing the children of Israel — or the Church — or the individual on the way to perfection, and in particular a section of chapter 5.

> 2 I sleep but my heart is awake.
>   A sound! My beloved is knocking!
>   Open to me, my sister, my companion,
>   my dove, my perfect one,
>   for my head is full of dew,
>   my locks with the drops of the night.
> 3 I have put off my tunic,
>   how shall I put it on?
>   I have washed my feet,
>   how shall I defile them?

---

[*] See also Edmée Kingsmill SLG, *The Song of Songs and the Eros of God: A Study in Biblical Intertextuality* (Oxford University Press, 2009).

> 4 My beloved put his hand through the opening
>   and my inward parts were moved for him.
> 5 I rose up to open to my beloved,
>   and my hands dripped with myrrh,
>   my fingers with flowing myrrh,
>   upon the handles of the bolt.
> 6 I opened to my beloved,
>   but my beloved had turned and gone.
>   My soul went forth at his departing.
>   I sought him, but I found him not;
>   I called him, but he did not answer me.
> 7 The watchmen who go about the city found me,
>   they smote me, they wounded me;
>   the keepers of the walls
>   took my veil from me.

'I sleep but my heart is awake.' This highly compressed half-verse reveals the poet to be one experienced in contemplative prayer which explains the Song's resonance with those who pray similarly. Gregory of Nyssa, the fourth-century Church Father who wrote one of the great commentaries on the Song of Songs, gives us a description of this state:

> We see in the bride a new paradoxical mixture of the opposites. 'I sleep', she says, 'but my heart is awake.' What can we understand by this statement? This sleep is like death. In it each sensory function of the body is lost: there is no vision, hearing, scent, taste, nor feeling, but the body's tension is loosed. Once all the senses have been put to sleep and are gripped by inaction, the heart's action is pure; reason looks above while it remains undisturbed and free from the senses' movement.[54]

Similarly the great Antony of the Egyptian desert in the early fourth century taught that: 'prayer is not perfect in the course of which the monk knows he is praying'. Evagrius, also a monk of the Egyptian desert, rather later than Antony, evidently knew the same

---

[54] Gregory of Nyssa, *Commentary on the Song of Songs*, trans. with an introduction by Casimir McCambley OCSO (Hellenic College Press, 1987).

state. He writes in his *Chapters on Prayer*: 'Happy the soul which attains to total insensibility at prayer.'[55] Teresa of Ávila, that great analyst of states of prayer, refers frequently to this state in her *Meditations on the Song of Songs*:

> Indeed the soul does not even find itself awake in order to love. But blessed sleep, happy inebriation that makes the Bridegroom supply what the soul cannot do, for while the faculties are dead or asleep, love remains alive.[56]

What seems clear from these writers is that the soul does not know what is going on in it when the faculties are held in prayer because, as St Theresa writes, the faculties are dead or asleep. There are three places in the Song where, it seems, the same state is referred to. They are all identical, but the first and the third are preceded by what may be seen as the reason for the state:

> His left hand is under my head, and his right hand embraces me.
> I adjure you, O daughters of Jerusalem,
> by the gazelles or by the harts of the field,
> that you stir not up nor awaken love 'til it please.

This verse occurs at 2:7, 3:5, and 8:4.[57] The 'daughters of Jerusalem' may be understood as the population of Jerusalem which here, as frequently, is personified as the mother. But 'daughters' can also be a metaphor for the nations, and we will come to an example of this meaning later in our passage. The gazelles and the harts are immensely important and we will look into what they might mean later.

---

[55] Evagrius Ponticus, *Praktikos: Chapters on Prayer*, trans. John Eudes Bamberger OCSO, Cistercian Studies 4 (Cistercian Publications, 1970), 75, n. 54.

[56] Teresa of Ávila, *The Collected Works. Volume 2: The Way of Perfection, Meditations on the Song of Songs, The Interior Castle*, trans. Kieran Kavanagh OCD and Otilio Rodriguez OCD (Institute of Carmelite Studies, 1980), 252.

[57] The clearest account known to me of the pain caused to someone by being disturbed when in this state of prayer is a description in John Saward, *Perfect Fools* (Oxford University Press, 1980), 201–2, of a well-meaning lady arousing from deep prayer the beggar-saint Benedict-Joseph Labre in order to invite him to dinner.

After the line, 'I sleep, but my heart is awake', the bride exclaims: 'A sound! My beloved is knocking!' Then the beloved speaks: 'Open to me, my sister, my companion, my dove, my perfect one, for my head is full of dew, my locks with the drops of the night.' It seems that although the bride is 'asleep' in prayer, and has consequently drawn the beloved to her door, he is complaining of being kept out. And her reply confirms this impression: 'I have put off my tunic, how shall I put it on? I have washed my feet, how shall I defile them?' The bride interprets the request to open the door as a threat to her state of hard-won purity. 'I have put off my tunic, how shall I put it on?'

The vocabulary of this line takes us back to the story of the Fall in the third chapter of Genesis. After the punishments are meted out first to the serpent, then to the woman and finally to the man, there comes the concluding sentence: 'The Lord God made garments of skin, and he clothed them.' The word 'garment' in the Genesis line is the same as 'tunic' in the Song, and 'clothed' in Genesis is the same word as 'put on' in her question, 'How shall I put it on?' The word for 'skin' in Genesis, although clearly in the singular, is always translated in the plural which effectively obscures what is actually being done to Adam and Eve.

The 'tunics of skin' are understood to represent an alteration of state from bodies which enjoyed incorporeality and were destined for immortality, to bodies confined in a corporeal structure and subject to mortality. These were understood in early Christianity to have been cast off by the sacrifice of Christ, and our original nature revealed by his capacity after the resurrection to enjoy the benefits of both incorporeality and corporeality (cf. the Resurrection appearances where Jesus passes through locked doors and—at Luke 24:43—eats a piece of broiled fish). A study, 'The Garments of Skin in Apocryphal Narrative and Biblical Commentary',[58] explores early exegesis of Genesis 3:21 and finds that the punishments inflicted on Adam and Eve in the verses leading up to the final punishment of being clothed in skin at 3:21, were understood as 'specific penitential

---

[58] Gary Anderson in *Studies in Ancient Midrash*, ed. James Kugel (Harvard University Press, 2001), 101–43.

disciplines intended to counterbalance the decree of death imposed on the body'. In the light of discoveries in modern times which reveal that Jewish asceticism flourished in the pre-Christian centuries we are able to speculate that long before Christian ascetics 'practised penitential disciplines imposed on the body', the implication of 'I have taken off my tunic' is that Jewish ascetics were doing the same. It seems likely, then, that the poet was one of those ascetics, which would account for the role played by the Song of Songs in the history of monasticism.

The author of the Song is, it seems to me, addressing those who envisage that a life of sufficient virtue can achieve the casting off of the 'tunic of skin'. But he disabuses such a hope by going on to indicate that there yet remains a covering on the bride which can only be removed by others, by the watchmen, as he calls them. The claim made next by the bride, that she has washed her feet and cannot be expected to defile them, seems also to belong to the poet's view that rising up in response to love's demands and not settling down with ideas of perfection is what is being asked of her. St Augustine, in his commentary on the Gospel of John, uses this line in a heading: 'How the Church fears to defile her feet on the way to Christ.'

In the next two lines we see the bride aroused by the action of the beloved: 'My beloved put his hand through the opening and my inward parts were moved for him.' The words $m\bar{e}'im$ (bowels, belly, the seat of the emotions), translated here 'inward parts', and $h\bar{a}m\bar{a}$ (murmur, growl, to be moved), occur together in two other places. At Isaiah 16:11, in an oracle against Moab, God declares: 'Therefore my inward parts are moved like a lyre for Moab.' At Jeremiah 31:2 God is troubled for Ephraim: 'Therefore my inward parts are moved for him.' A third occurrence in a manuscript from the Cairo Genizah of the Hebrew of Sirach 61 includes both 'my inward parts were moved' and 'my hand opened' in a hymn which is about the love of the soul for wisdom.

Then, in the words of the bride: 'I rose up to open to my beloved, and my hands dripped with myrrh, my fingers with flowing myrrh, upon the handles of the bolt.' The scene is, I think, more redolent of eros than any other in the Song, moving the reader at one level or another by language and imagery which touches the 'inward parts' with a sense of extraordinary intimacy—whether at the level of human eros or that of Eivine Eros depends, of course, on the nature of the reader.

Myrrh is closely related to a number of nouns denoting 'bitterness'. It seems that if myrrh in its eight occurrences in the Song is accompanied by frankincense, then it refers to the holy anointing oil, but if it occurs alone, as here, it relates to words meaning 'bitter' and, consequently, to suffering.

> I opened to my beloved—
> but my beloved had turned and gone.
> My soul went forth at his departing.
> I sought him, but I found him not;
> I called him but he did not answer me. (Song 5:6)

The themes of seeking and finding, or not finding, of calling and being answered, or not being answered, occur in many contexts, but the books which provide the most examples in relation to God are the Psalms, Isaiah and Jeremiah. 'He will call me and I will answer him' (Ps. 91:15). In Isaiah it is God who calls, but there is no answer (50:2; 65:12; 66:4), and similarly in Jeremiah: 'I called you, but you did not answer' (7:13). Or God declares that Israel will seek him but will not find him (Hos. 5:6). Wisdom declares the same thing: 'Then they will call upon me, but I will not answer; they will seek me diligently but will not find me' (Prov. 1:28). Or, again, God declares that Israel will seek him: 'Then you will call upon me and come and pray to me, and I will hear you. You will seek me and find me when you seek me with all your heart, I will be found by you, says the Lord' (Jer. 29:12–14a). Examples abound. The bride continues:

> The watchmen who go about the city found me;
> they smote me, they wounded me;
> the keepers of the walls
> took my veil from me. (Song 5:7)

The function of the watchmen is unique to the Song in the biblical books, but there are one or two resonances elsewhere, the most important being that at Isaiah 62:6: 'I have set watchmen upon your walls, O Jerusalem, which shall never hold their peace day nor night.' These watchmen are, I think, to be identified with the watchmen in the Song who rob the bride of her veil.

The word *rādid*, meaning 'large veil', 'wide wrapper', or 'female garment' occurs only twice in the Old Testament, at Isaiah 3:23, and here in the Song. The passage in Isaiah is a particularly virulent example of the castigation of the female principle. That is to say, it is *not* in my view a castigation of women. It is, I believe, a mistake to understand men and women in the Old Testament in terms of gender: The daughters of Zion here should be distinguished from the daughters of Jerusalem. Zion, in the poetic books, usually stands for the Temple. It is, therefore, very probable that Isaiah intends the priests in this passage, for they frequently come under condemnation by the prophets.

Whereas the bride shows the feminine principle in its positive aspect, which includes the reflective, the creative, the practical, the contemplative, here the feminine principle is shown in its negative aspect, that of luxuriating in self pleasing, self-seeking, especially of spiritual sensation. Here are a few lines from the passage:

> In that day the Lord will take away the finery of the anklets,
>   the headbands and the crescents;
> the pendants, the bracelets and the scarves;
> the head-dresses, the armlets, the sashes, the perfume boxes,
>   and the amulets;
> the signet rings and nose rings;
> the festal robes, the mantles, the cloaks, and the handbags;
> the garments of gauze, the linen garments, the turbans,
>   and the veils.   (Is. 3:18–23)

The particular point to note here is that the last item of which the daughters of Zion are stripped are their veils. Likewise in the Song, the watchmen strike the bride as she searches for the beloved, and strip her of her veil, her last bulwark, the use of the word implies, against total vulnerability, and which is hindering perfect union with the beloved. Then the bride, now stripped of all protection, appeals to the daughters of Jerusalem:

> I charge you, O daughters of Jerusalem,
> if you find my beloved,
> what will you tell him?
> [Tell him] that I am faint from love.
> Then the daughters of Jerusalem ask her:
> What is your beloved more than another beloved,
> O fairest among women?
> What is your beloved more than another beloved,
> that you so charge us?   (Song 5:8–9)

Here the daughters of Jerusalem seem to stand for the nations, which is how the Midrash on the Song of Songs understands this verse: 'The other nations say to Israel: What is thy beloved more than another beloved? What is thy God more than other gods?' The word for 'beloved' in the Song is *dod* which only occurs otherwise at Isaiah 5:1 where it clearly means God: 'Let me sing for my beloved my love-song concerning his vineyard …' Isaiah 5:1ff. is the key which unlocks the meaning of the Song, a subject which requires a chapter in itself.

The bride, now perfected through suffering, is able to give a picture of the one 'whom my soul loves' (Song 1:7). The long passage which follows is her description which concludes: 'This is my beloved, and this is my friend, O daughters of Jerusalem.' Thus we come to the subject of our second part.

II

THE BELOVED

Modern scholarship on the Song of Songs has been obliged, given the consensus on this biblical book, to treat the description of the male at 5:10–16 as being that of a human figure. But comparisons with descriptions in other parts of the Bible and with pseudepigraphical literature show that, far from being a human lover, this passage describes the divine *kavod* ('the glory of God'), or the Messiah, which goes back to the Second Temple period. Here is the passage which is the description of him given by the bride in chapter 5:

> 10 My beloved is radiant and ruddy
>   exalted above ten thousand.
> 11 His head is the most fine gold;
>   his locks are bushy,
>   and black as a raven.
> 12 His eyes are like doves
>   by streams of waters;
>   bathed in milk, fitly set.
> 13 His cheeks are like terraces of spices,
>   yielding perfumes.
>   His lips are lilies,
>   dripping with flowing myrrh.
> 14 His hands are cylinders of gold
>   set with tarshish;
>   his loins are panels of ivory
>   overlaid with sapphires;
> 15 his legs are pillars of marble
>   set upon pillars of gold.
>   His appearance is like Lebanon,
>   chosen like cedars.
> 16 His speech is exceedingly sweet,
>   and all of him is most precious.
>   This is my beloved, and this is my friend,
>   O daughters of Jerusalem. (Song 5:10–16)

The detail in this passage is—or should be—such as to silence any commentator who wants to see this passage as describing a human lover. The first two lines lead us from one theophany or apocalypse to another. The combination of 'radiant and ruddy', or 'red and white' occurs widely, from ancient to more modern times, especially in myths and fairy tales. One ancient example comes from 1 Enoch, an important work among the pseudepigrapha which has many links with the Song:

> And after some days my son, Methuselah, took a wife for his son Lamech, and she became pregnant and bore him a son. And his body was white as snow and red as the blooming of a rose, and the hair of his head and his long locks were white as wool, and his eyes beautiful. (1 Enoch 106:1–3)

This description recalls David: 'And he was ruddy, with beautiful eyes' (1 Sam. 16:12). There is much more on the subject of being red, ruddy, or like fire, fiery, and we shall see some examples. The next two words are, 'exalted above myriads', or 'distinguished above ten thousand'. The word *rĕvāvā*, multitude, myriad, ten thousand (in an indefinite sense), occurs sixteen times in the Old Testament. The following comes from the blessing of Moses before his death:

> The Lord came from Sinai,
> and dawned from Seir for us;
> he shone forth from Mount Paran;
> he came from myriads of holy ones;
> from his right hand a fiery law for us. (Deut. 33:2)

The book of Daniel resonates powerfully with the Song. One passage to which the Song passage is seen to relate, especially in the rabbinic literature, is that at 7:9–10:

> As I watched, thrones were set in place,
> and the Ancient of Days took his throne;
> his clothing was white as snow,
> and the hair of his head like pure wool;
> his throne was fiery flames,
> and its wheels were burning fire.
> A stream of fire issued
> and flowed out from his presence.
> A thousand thousand served him,
> and ten thousand times ten thousand stood before him …

Another passage in Daniel also has links to the Song:

> I lifted up my eyes and looked, and behold, a man clothed in linen, whose loins were girded with gold of Uphaz. His body was like *tarshish*, his face like the appearance of lightning, his eyes like flaming torches, his arms and legs like the gleam of burnished bronze …
> (Dan. 10:5–6)

The phrase 'gold of Uphaz' is linked here to the loins and not to the head as in the Song. The word *tarshish*—usually translated 'beryl', although we do not know what it means—is used in the description of the beloved and in the description of the four living creatures at Ezekiel 1:16. And at Ezekiel 1:26ff. there is a throne over their heads:

> in appearance like sapphire [a word always present in theophanies], and seated above the likeness of a throne was a likeness of a human form, and upward from what had the appearance of his loins I saw as it were gleaming bronze, like the appearance of fire enclosed round about; and downward from what had the appearance of his loins, I saw as it were the appearance of fire …

Compare the description of the beloved;

> His hands are gold cylinders
>   set with tarshish;
> his loins are panels of ivory,
>   overlaid with sapphires …   (Song 5:14)

There is a passage at 1 Enoch 46:1–3, which links closely with Daniel 7:

> And I saw one who had a head of days,
>   and His head was like white wool,
> and with him was another being whose countenance
>   had the appearance of a man.
> And his face was full of graciousness,
>   like one of the holy angels.

The passage continues in prose:

> And I asked the angel who went with me and showed me all the hidden things concerning the Son of Man, who he was and whence he was, and why he went with the Head of Days? And he answered and said to me:
> This is the Son of Man who has righteousness,
>   with whom dwells righteousness,
> and who reveals all the treasures of that which is hidden,
>   because the Lord of Spirits has chosen him.

This last line links to the opening verse of the bride's praise of the beloved translated here 'exalted above ten thousand', and by the Septuagint 'having been chosen above myriads'. Finally, from the passages linked by vocabulary to all these theophanic texts is that at Revelation 1:12–16 where there is a vision which evidently belongs in the same tradition:

I saw seven golden lampstands, and in the midst of the lampstands one like a son of man, clothed with a long robe and with a golden girdle round his breast; his head and his hair were white as white wool, white as snow; his eyes were like a flame of fire, his feet were like burnished bronze, refined as in a furnace, and his voice was like the sound of many waters ... and his face was like the sun shining in full strength.

The hair as white as wool in all these passages is the detail which is in contrast to the beloved whose 'locks are bushy and black as a raven' conveying a picture of powerful youth. But, as we have seen, there is no simple equation, black hair = youth, and white hair = age, since the white wool hair is ascribed to the child born to Lamech, while even more difficult from the standpoint of the speculation that the beloved represents the 'son of man' figure is the passage in Revelation which ascribes to him 'hair white as white wool, white as snow'. But in a pseudepigraphical work, *Joseph and Asenath,* Joseph is described as having a head 'all white as snow' while at the same time 'the hairs of his head were exceedingly close and thick like those of an Ethopian', that is, black. This is very close to: 'His head is the most fine gold, his locks bushy and black as a raven' and suggests a tradition which ascribes both the black hair of youth and the white hair of wisdom to a theophanic figure, a tradition also found in the Talmud;

> One verse says: His raiment was white as snow, and the hair of his head like pure wool (Daniel 7:9) and [the other] His locks are curled and black as a raven (Song 5:11). There is no contradiction: one verse refers to God in session, and the other to God in war.[59]

Nevertheless, the frequency of the figures with hair white as wool does suggest some difference of aspect between them and the beloved, and a greater knowledge of the mighty literature on the pseudepigrapha and apocalypses might reveal what the difference means. But I hope the examples I have given, which locate the passage in praise of the beloved among its evident relations, provides sufficient grounds for seeing the figure in the Song as an aspect of the

---

[59] From b. Hagigah 14a.

kavod—the Divine Glory—which emerged in the thought world of the last centuries before the Christian era, with one example from that era—Revelation—which suggests the destination of this particular strand of tradition to which we now come.

*

> Flee, my beloved,
>   and be like a gazelle
> or a young hart
>   upon the mountains of spices.   (Song 8:14)

This verse, the last in the Song, is spoken by the bride who here represents the figure of Wisdom. She is telling the beloved to flee and to be like a gazelle or a young hart. What is the significance of these two animals together?

The gazelle and the hart are paired seven times in the Song. A search for the source of these creatures reveals two: Deuteronomy and 1 Kings. In chapters 12, 14 and 15 of Deuteronomy the gazelle and the hart occur in four verses:

> With all the desire of your soul, you may sacrifice and eat flesh in all your gates according to the blessing of the Lord your God which he has given to you; the unclean and the clean may eat of it, as of the gazelle and as of the hart.   (Deut. 12:15)

> As the gazelle and the hart is eaten, so you may eat of it; the unclean and the clean together may eat of it.   (Deut. 12:15)

> These are the animals you may eat: the ox, the sheep, the goat; the hart and the gazelle, the roebuck, the wild goat, the ibex, the antelope, and the mountain-sheep.   (Deut. 14:4–5)

> you shall eat it within your gates; the unclean and the clean together, like the gazelle and like the hart.   (Deut. 15:22).

The context of the verse at 1 Kings 4:23, is a description of the provision of food made each day for Solomon—the putative author of the Song: 'Ten fat oxen, and twenty oxen out of the pastures, and an hundred sheep, beside harts, and roebucks, and gazelles, and fatted fowl'.

How then might we understand this last verse when the female exhorts the beloved to go and to be like a gazelle or a young hart?[60] The ineluctable conclusion to be drawn in my view is that the beloved is being exhorted to go and to be food. But where and for whom? If we see the bride as perfected Israel and a Wisdom figure here, then her exhortation to the beloved, that is, to the Messiah, is made from the perspective of heaven. Go, she says, and be food for the world. And so a messiah is born in Bethlehem—*beit lechem*—the house of bread, and is laid in a manger, that is, in a trough in a stable from which cattle eat. And this messiah declares: 'I am the living bread which came down from heaven. whoever eats this bread will live for ever' (John 6:51). And at the Last Supper in another Gospel this same man took bread, and blessed, and broke it, and gave it to the disciples, and said, 'Take, eat, this is my body' (Matthew 26:26), which is done at every Eucharist when the priest holds up the consecrated wafer and, quoting John 1:29 and 36, says: 'Behold the Lamb of God, who takes away the sin of the world', after which he distributes it to the congregation to be eaten.

These texts are not, of course, adduced because I believe the poet foresaw them but because they manifest the realization of his understanding of wisdom as food, an understanding clearly articulated by Ben Sira who, in the figure of Wisdom declares: 'Those who eat me will hunger for more, and those who drink me will thirst for more.' (Sir. 24:21). The poet, no less a wisdom writer than Sirach, sends the messiah he eagerly awaits into the world to be wisdom for the world and therefore to be its food. The gazelle and the hart are to be eaten 'by the unclean and the clean together', as would, indeed, happen from the earliest days of Christianity.

This brings us to the problem of who it is who represents Wisdom in the biblical books. In the first nine chapters of Proverbs, and in the Deuterocanonical books, the Wisdom of Solomon, and

---

[60] The verb 'to flee' can also mean 'to go/pass through'. I have retained the usual translation, 'to flee', but 'to go/to pass through' namely the heavens, is, I believe, the most likely interpretation.

Sirach, Wisdom is hypostasized as female. Similarly in the Song there are moments when the female appears as the figure of Wisdom:

> Who is she who looks down like the morning star,
>   fair as the moon, bright as the sun,
>   terrible as the bannered hosts? (Song 6:10)

In the New Testament it is the male figure, Jesus, who is seen in a number of key texts to be 'the wisdom of God', and these texts have formed our understanding from that time to the present. Nevertheless, in the Latin tradition of the West, Mary has shared this role as we can see from the liturgical texts for her feasts, largely taken from Sirach 24, *the* wisdom chapter above all others.

However, the final verse of the Song reveals the beloved to be the uncreated figure of Wisdom. We have seen him linked to several theophanies, both biblical and pseudepigraphic, and thus we were prepared to understand him as the Messiah who was to come. But to see him also as the figure of Wisdom, despatched by Wisdom to be Wisdom incarnate, brings the vision which inspired the author of the Song even closer to the Christian understanding of the figure depicted in the New Testament, and fully justifies early Christian interpretations which saw the bridegroom of the Song as the anticipation of the bridegroom of the Gospels. A modern Russian theologian, Bulgakov, took a similar view of the Song writing that:

> the essential meaning of this mysterious hymn of love becomes comprehensible because of the teaching of the New Testament about the Church, since in truth this song from the Old Testament forms the most New Testament part of the canon ... everything is accomplished in the Song of Songs.[61]

Yes, indeed. In the portrayal of life as it was originally intended to be, and in its reversal of how it had become, all is wonderfully accomplished. Yet the last line of the Song suggests that the accomplishment

---

[61] Protopresbyter Sergii Bulgakov, *Kupina Neopalimaya* (YMCA Press, 1927), 187; trans. Boris Jakim, *Sergius Bulgakov, The Friend of the Bridegroom* (Eerdmans, 2003).

is just about to begin. The realization of the perfection portrayed depends on the beloved 'going through' the heavens to become 'food' for the world. And what that would mean is portrayed by a later poet, a Jewish Christian, probably second century AD, who wrote *The Odes of Solomon*. Apart from the attribution to the father of sapiential writing, namely, Solomon, there are many points of contact between the two poets. But the Odist lived after the beloved had become food for the world and thus he knew what it had cost:

> ... I bore their bitterness because of humility;
> In order that I might deliver my people and
>   take possession of them,
> And that I might not render void the promises
>   to the patriarchs,
> For the deliverance of whose seed I was promised.[62]

Finally, of the many lines which might be chosen to show the impact of the Messiah on the author of the *Odes of Solomon*, as well as links with the eros of God in the Song of Songs here, in conclusion, are a few lines from the last ode, Ode 42:

> I have laid upon them the yoke of my love.
> As the arm of the bridegroom upon the bride,
> So is my yoke on those who know me;
> And as the bed that is spread in the bridal chamber.
> So is my love upon those who believe in me.

---

[62] J. A. Emerton, ed. and trans., 'The Odes of Solomon', in *The Apocryphal Old Testament*, ed. H. F. D. Sparks (Clarendon Press, 1984), 721. The last line is Emerton's alternative in a footnote to the line he provides in the text: 'Whose seed I promised to deliver.'

ON BRINGING A RIGHT SPIRIT TO THE OLD TESTAMENT

And [Elisha] went up from there to Beth-el; and as he was going up in the way, little children came forth from the city and mocked him, saying to him: 'Go up, baldhead! Go up baldhead!' And he turned round and looked at them, and he cursed them in the name of the Lord. And there came forth two she-bears out of the wood, and they tore in pieces forty-two of the children.   (2 Kings 2:23–4).

Well, you will be thinking, what hope is there of bringing a right spirit to that charming story! I was reminded of it in a recent conversation with an Old Testament scholar who mentioned it as an example of the savagery of the Old Testament in comparison with the New, and he cited Luke 9:52ff. where the Samaritans refuse to welcome Jesus, and James and John ask: 'Lord, do you want us to command fire to come down from heaven and consume them?' The reply attributed to Jesus is evidently thought to be a Christian gloss for it is now relegated to a footnote which informs us that 'Other ancient authorities read, "as Elijah did"',[63] and goes on to give Jesus's rebuke: 'You do not know what manner of spirit you are of; for the Son of man came not to destroy men's lives but to save them.' Old Testament scholars understood this to imply a reproach of the Old Testament way of settling one's enemies, and at the time I could only agree with him, and thought no more about it.

But the next morning I found an interpretation emerging from another level of consciousness. I dimly recalled an incident in my teens when I was with another girl somewhere or other, and we were both

---

[63] Probably referring to the episode involving the captain of fifty in 2 Kings 1:9–16.

laughing immoderately, I cannot recall about what. But our stupid laughter attracted to us a man who became a menace, and I remember our becoming alarmed. Presumably we got rid of him, and the incident is in no way a parallel to the Elisha story. But it gave me a clue. If the sneering, mocking child in us laughs at a holy man on his way up to the house of God—which is what Bethel means—then we are laying our souls open to be savaged by forces too strong for us.

I cannot explain the story better than that, but the point I want to make is that the interpretation, and the conviction that the story is not to be read literally, emerged from another level of consciousness. We are all familiar with the idea of two levels of consciousness, the conscious mind and the unconscious, but there is a third level, rarely recognized because, unlike the first two, it has to be developed by prayer, or by some form of creative activity which is directed to this level of consciousness and not to that of ordinary consciousness—much less to all those activities which are unconsciously motivated. We can call this third level the 'supra-conscious'. It is a level we must all share, since we would not be here if we were not people who pray, and who desire above all to increase this level of consciousness. And on its development, I believe, depends the capacity to read the Bible in accordance with a kind of reading we know as *lectio divina*, traditionally practised by those living the monastic life, but by no means confined to such.[64]

Now the problem of how we read the Old Testament may not be an issue for any of us here, but it is a problem for the Church and has been from the beginning. In the early days the culmination of the Scriptures revealed in the incarnation of Christ produced giants like Tertullian, Irenaeus, Clement, Origen, and others who all taught the unity of the two Testaments, and whose depth of understanding, both of what was amazingly new in Christ but also what was amazingly profound in the Scriptures which led up to Him, enabled them to

---

[64] Clement of Alexandria, in the third century, taught that the path to the knowledge of God lies through the study of the Bible but, uniquely for his time, he considered marriage to be the preferred state for the attainment of perfection.

combat the influence of powerful heretics who attracted followers in those first centuries.

Of these early heretics Marcion has proved the most dangerous because he represents the Christian mind when it is undeveloped in the spiritual insight necessary for reading the Bible, especially the Old Testament. Consequently, his influence emerged once again when mystical theology ran out of steam in the early Renaissance period. Anything left of its spirit was, in general terms, finished by the Reformation on both sides of the divide—though not before Spain had produced its swansong in the teaching of the two great Carmelites, and German Lutheranism had produced Bach and the librettists who provided mystical texts for much of his music, as well as extraordinary exceptions like Ann Griffiths, and a number of others down to recent times. There are, thank God, always exceptions who are not bound by the spirit of the times. Nevertheless, as the spirit of humanism, which enabled the Reformation, yielded to the rationalism of the Enlightenment, religious thought in the West became dominated by the thought processes of the ordinary conscious mind. In such a climate Marcion was bound to re-emerge. Let us look at him first in his second-century setting, and then at his re-emergence in the hands of a German theologian in the early twentieth century.

Marcion was a Greek who, about 140, went to Rome where he worked out his system and organized his followers into a separate community to mainstream Christians, leading in 144 to his formal excommunication.[65] He was considered a heretic because he insisted on a separation between the severe and cruel 'creator' God of the Jews and the Christian God of love as revealed in Christ. In his system the revelation of God through Christ should replace, not fulfil, the Scriptures, and the two 'testaments' had no relation to each other. Any New Testament writings that did not support his view were simply rejected as fabrications.

This, then, is the heretic who was taken up by the famous Church historian, Adolf von Harnack, 1851–1930. John O'Neill, in his book

---

[65] Blackman, *Marcion and his Influence*, 8.

The Bible's Authority, which brilliantly charts the downward course of rational religious thinking in German theology, has a chapter on Harnack in which he writes:

> In all the upheaval of the post-war years, [Harnack] produced a major study on the second-century heretic Marcion, which is still the standard book on the subject. He brought to fruition the work begun in the essay on Marcion's teaching with which he won a gold medal as a nineteen-year-old student of the University of Dorpat, the work which in his speech on taking up membership of the Berlin Academy in 1890 he said remained the real object of all his research. He argued that Marcion was as great a reformer of the Church as Luther. Marcion attempted to recover the true teaching of Jesus and Paul about the God of love who was above the God of wrath of the Old Testament.[66]

Harnack was extraordinarily influential in his day. O'Neill tells us that Harnack 'learnt a sweet and patient tolerance of those who felt Christianity itself was threatened by his arguments',[67] especially following the break with his father, a distinguished Lutheran theologian, who wrote a tragic letter to the young Adolf after the publication of Volume I of his *Lehrbuch der Dogmengeschichte*, or *History of Dogma*:

> Our difference is not merely theological but a profound and directly Christian difference, so that if I overlooked it I should be betraying Christ, and no one, not even someone who stands so near to me as you, my son, could demand that of me or expect it. To name only the all-decisive issue: whoever regards the fact of the resurrection as you do is in my eyes no longer a Christian theologian.[68]

O'Neill ends his chapter by describing Harnack as the 'perfect servant of whatever comes to pass, the highly educated functionary who makes our modern world go wherever it is going'. And where Harnack's world was going was into the world of Hitler, and what he unwittingly helped to enable was the liquidation of those for whom the Bible is that rejected by Marcionism.

---

[66] John C. O'Neill, *The Bible's Authority: A Portrait Gallery of Thinkers from Lessing to Bultmann* (T&T Clark, 1991), 223.
[67] O'Neill, *The Bible's Authority*, 218.
[68] Quoted in O'Neill, *The Bible's Authority*, 217.

Harnack's book on Marcion was never translated into English, but the book I have already referred to by Anders Nygren, *Agape and Eros*, was and, one might say, filled the gap. The first part appeared in English in 1932, the second in 1938 and a revision of the whole in one volume in 1953. It was widely read and, in its view that agape is all good and eros is all bad, was enormously influential on theologians such as Barth, Tillich, Niebuhr and many others. Nygren's concern is to untie the knot which had, in more than a thousand-year-old tradition, kept eros and agape bound together, while an allied theme is to untie the knot between the two Testaments. Thus, on Harnack's view of Marcion, Nygren writes:

> Harnack's monograph on Marcion describes him as incomparably the most significant religious personality between Paul and Augustine. Without further qualification this judgement perhaps contains a measure of exaggeration; but with specific reference to the history of the Christian idea of love, there is probably no other between Paul and Augustine who could rival Marcion in importance.[69]

Nygren, however, is not entirely uncritical of Marcion, but he serves his cause by highlighting the distinction between Law and Love on which point he believes Marcion was right. And if there is no love in the Old Testament, then the beautiful paean of praise which describes the love between God and his creation that lies at its heart, the Song of Songs, must be understood as concerning a pair of human lovers. Nygren only refers to the Song once:

> we need hardly mention the disastrous part played by the mystical interpretation of the Song of Songs in assisting the identification of the Eros motif with the Christian idea of Agape.[70]

It would be difficult to overestimate the damaging influence of Nygren's combination of learning and compelling air of verisimilitude, especially in our theological colleges where *Eros and Agape* became recommended reading after it had been made available in one volume in 1953.

---

[69] Nygren, *Agape and Eros*, 317.
[70] Nygren, *Agape and Eros*, 230.

In 1958 C. S. Lewis published a small, modest study called *Reflections on the Psalms*.[71] If it were possible to agree with his line, which is implicitly Marcionate throughout, one would delight in much of the book. The psychological acuity he brings to the different types of psalms viewed in purely human terms is often brilliant. But he makes the cardinal error of referring to the Old Testament as Jewish and, worse, frequently compares the Old Testament on this score to its disadvantage with the New. For instance: 'I think there are very good reasons for regarding the Christian picture of God's judgement as far more profound and far safer for our souls than the Jewish.'[72] There is an underlying patronising tone toward the writers of the Old Testament which, combined with the anachronistic use of Jew and Jewish, is subtly anti-Semitic. Lewis frequently reports the views of biblical scholars. Did not one of them tell him that terms like Judaism and Jewish cannot properly be used before the inter-testamental period? That Christians, no less than the Jews, *are* the Israelites of the biblical books?[73] Nevertheless, toward the end of the book Lewis produces some extraordinary insights, and I will return to one of them when we come to look at Psalm 137.

Now, the point of all this history is that in consequence of it, Marcionism is, alas!, very much around—especially among those who have never heard of this heresy. It has, so to speak, got into the bloodstream. I was at a large meeting of Jews and Christians at Leo Baeck College a few years ago in the course of which one of the Jewish participants related that he had recently been told by a Christian lady that the God of the Christians and the God of the Jews are different and that the God of the Christians is the God of love, while the God of the Jews is the God of wrath. This was followed by several others who reported similar experiences with Christians. This kind of thinking has insidiously become part of our assumptions with the result that the Old Testament is taken at face value, and understood at the level of ordinary

---

[71] C. S. Lewis, *Reflections on the Psalms* (G. Bles, 1958).
[72] Lewis, *Reflections on the Psalms*, 12.
[73] See the chapter above, 'The Bible, the Jews and the Spirit of Marcion', 18–19.

consciousness. This inevitably leads to the demand that we omit from our reading those passages which seem to bear out the view that the God of the Old Testament is the God of wrath. Read in this way the savagery of the Old Testament, taken literally, is held to be an element in the savagery of the treatment of the Jews by the Germans, and that on this account we may no longer use, in particular, the 'cursing psalms'. Thus, in the light of the Holocaust and by way of reparation to the Jews, we reinforce precisely that understanding of the Old Testament which contributed to their persecution in the first place.

Against all this we must assert the necessity of bringing faith and goodwill to the reading of the Old Testament. Let us return to the second century and draw from Clement of Alexandria two fundamental principles against Marcion—of whom he was a younger contemporary—as guides to biblical interpretation.[74] The first is that we can accept as literally true nothing that is unworthy of God, and second, that we can accept no interpretation which is inconsistent with the Bible as a whole.

Origen, Clement's great pupil, studied both Testaments with a passion for the letter no less than the spirit. Origen is widely thought of as an allegorizer, but although he does on occasion employ allegory, it is a misunderstanding to suppose allegory to be the method on which he relies. Far from it. His normal procedure is to study every word not only in the passage under consideration but wherever it has been used, a huge task without the benefit of our modern concordances. One example, which springs readily to mind because it comes in his great commentary on the Song of Songs, occurs at Song 1:2 where he interprets 'mouth'—'let him kiss me with the kisses of his mouth'—as being that into which words are poured: 'May he pour the words of his mouth into mine, that I may hear him speak himself.' Readers now assume he is allegorizing to avoid the sexual implications of the verse. But that is because they do not know that neither

---

[74] Clement of Alexandria, *The Stromata*, trans. William Wilson, in *Ante-Nicene Fathers*, vol. 2, ed. Alexander Roberts, James Donaldson, and A. Cleveland Coxe (Christian Literature Publishing Co.,1885).

verb nor noun of 'kiss' is ever used of lovers' kisses in the biblical literature, and that his interpretation of 'mouth' as being that into which words are poured is amply borne out by biblical usage, as the following typical examples show:

Speak unto him and put words in his mouth	(Ex. 4:15)
The word which God puts in my mouth	(Num. 22:38)
The Lord put a word in Balaam's mouth	(Num. 23:5)
That which the Lord has put in my mouth	(Num. 23:12)
I ... will put my words in his mouth, and he shall speak unto them all that I shall command him	(Deut. 18:18)
He has put a new song in my mouth	(Ps. 40:3)

Let us apply this way of studying a text to the notorious conclusion to Psalm 137, which I have already mentioned above (p. 29):

> Blessed be the one who takes your little ones and dashes them against the rock! (Ps 137:9)

Naturally, if we have faith and goodwill we will ask ourselves whether 'little ones' are to be understood literally as 'little children' or, worse, 'babies'? And whether there can exist circumstances, however exceptional, which would justify declaring someone 'blessed' who takes tiny tots and dashes out their brains? And here I am not so much thinking of the tots as of those who would perpetrate such a crime. For the little ones it would be a question of a moment's agony and then of being swept into the arms of their heavenly Father. For the perpetrator the outlook is black, unrelievedly so if he is motivated by self-righteousness, by a conviction of being blessed in the doing. Can those Scriptures, which all the truly great commentators have ardently believed to be inspired by the Holy Spirit, instruct us thus? And do we so fail in faith as to read them so? Let us, then, look carefully at the context, and at how the words in this verse are used.

First of all, the context is that of the tragedy of exile, especially exile from being able to sing the praises of God, 'for how shall we sing the Lord's song in a strange land?' The word for 'strange' here, *neicar*, is most often used in conjunction with foreign gods, thus: 'How shall we sing the Lord's song in the midst of idolatry?' The last two verses, which are a direct address to Babylon personified, desire that her little ones, *olelim*, will be dashed in pieces. The word occurs at Psalm 8:3 in a well-known metaphorical sense: 'Out of the mouths of babes and sucklings.' And that *olelim* should be dashed in pieces occurs in four other places: 2 Kings 8:12; Hosea 14:1; Nahum 3:10, and Isaiah 13:16, at which last the 'mother' is again Babylon. The word *olel*, 'little ones' here, is generally used as a metaphor for what a people or a city has given birth to, usually evil of some kind, which, in the prophets, means idolatry. Here the 'little ones' represent false worship, that is—to a devout Israelite—the lies, to which the 'daughter of Babylon' gives birth, and it is of such 'little ones' that a state of blessedness would be granted to the one who dashes them against the rock. But this interpretation depends on seeing that the word for 'rock' (*sela*) is a metaphor for God. It is explicitly so in 2 Samuel 22:2 and four Psalms in each of which the psalmist refers to God as a rock: Psalms 18:2, 31:3, 42:9 and 71:3). In Psalm 137 the psalmist is not talking explicitly, but does give a strong clue by providing the definite article. So it is not any old rock against which the *olelim* must be dashed; it is *the* rock, the one, true God, against whom all lies and false worship are to be dashed. Finally, having studied certain significant words in their different contexts, we find the key in yet another Psalm: 'Behold those who are in labour with wickedness, who conceive evil and give birth to lies.' (Ps. 7:14).

So this is the metaphorical language of the biblical literature. As you see, it requires drawing out by careful study, though in our day it is enormously facilitated by the excellent concordances available. You will also understand that this is not allegorizing; there is no attempt to impose a meaning which may or may not be what the biblical writer had in mind. It is an attempt to discover exactly what the biblical writer did have in mind. And what is unexpected is the surprising consistency with which the vocabulary is used.

This, then, is the way to study the Old Testament in particular. It is rarely, if ever, to be read literally. The biblical writers take images and symbols and use them for metaphors. Nevertheless, a reader may occasionally come up with an allegorical interpretation so brilliant that it deserves to be put alongside the metaphorical, and in this case C. S. Lewis has produced such a reading of the last two verses of Psalm 137. It worries me that he seems to think a literal reading could be the one intended by the psalmist, though I may be misreading him on this point. But here is his allegorization:

> ... I can use even the horrible passage in 137 about dashing the Babylonian babies against the stones [KJV mistranslation]. I know things in the inner world which are like babies; the infantile beginnings of small indulgences, small resentments, which may one day become dipsomania or settled hatred, but which woo us and wheedle us with special pleadings and seem so tiny, so helpless that in resisting them we feel we are being cruel to animals. They begin whimpering to us 'I don't ask much, but', or 'I had at least hoped', or 'you owe yourself *some* consideration'. Against all such pretty infants (the dears have such winning ways) the advice of the Psalm is the best. Knock the little bastards' brains out. And 'blessed' he who can, for it's easier said than done.[75]

Finally, I want to return to where we began, to the suggestion that the right spirit for the reading of the Old Testament is formed at the level of our supra-conscious mind, that level which is developed by prayer, especially that silent prayer which empties itself of ideas, opinions, judgements and the like in its desire to be filled with what is fresh from the Holy Spirit. There is a very great deal in the Old Testament which yields nothing to me in the way of a meaning beyond the surface meaning, but enough does yield a meaning for me to be sure that the fault is in myself. I have not allowed difficult passages to work on me, neither have I worked on them in the way described above. Until and unless I do, they will remain either repellent or closed to me.

---

[75] Lewis, *Reflections on the Psalms*, 136.

Bibliography

Anderson, Gary, 'The Garments of Skin in Apocryphal Narrative and Biblical Commentary', in *Studies in Ancient Midrash*, ed. James Kugel (Harvard University Press, 2001), 101–43.

St Augustine, *The Retractions*, trans. H. Browne, in *Nicene and Post-Nicene Fathers*, First Series, vol. 3, ed. Philip Schaff (Christian Literature Publishing Co., 1887).

Barton, John, *Oracles of God: Perceptions of Ancient Prophecy in Israel after the Exile* (Darton, Longman & Todd, 1986).

Blackman, Edwin C., *Marcion and his Influence* (SPCK, 1948).

Bulgakov, Protopresbyter Sergii, *Kupina Neopalimaya* (YMCA Press, 1927), trans. Boris Jakim, *Sergius Bulgakov, The Friend of the Bridegroom* (Eerdmans, 2003).

Clement of Alexandria, *The Stromata*, trans. William Wilson, in *Ante-Nicene Fathers*, vol. 2, ed. Alexander Roberts, James Donaldson, and A. Cleveland Coxe (Christian Literature Publishing Co., 1885).

Coggan, Donald, 'Jews and Christians', *Theology*, 93 (July, 1990), 261–6.

Cox, Harvey, *Many Mansions: A Christian's Encounter with Other Faiths* (Collins, 1988).

Emerton, J. A., ed. and trans., 'The Odes of Solomon', in *The Apocryphal Old Testament*, ed. H. F. D. Sparks (Clarendon Press, 1984).

Evagrius Ponticus, *Praktikos: Chapters on Prayer*, trans. John Eudes Bamberger OCSO, Cistercian Studies 4 (Cistercian Publications, 1970).

Feldman, Louis H., *Jew and Gentile in the Ancient World: Attitudes and Interactions from Alexander to Justinian* (Princeton University Press, 1993).

Green, Arthur, ed., *Jewish Spirituality* (Crossroad, 1987).

Green, Robin, *A Step too Far* (Darton, Longman & Todd, 1990).

Gregory of Nyssa, *Commentary on the Song of Songs*, trans. with an introduction by Casimir McCambley OCSO (Hellenic College Press, 1987).

Kingsmill, Edmée SLG, *The Song of Songs and the Eros of God: A Study in Biblical Intertextuality* (Oxford University Press, 2009).

Lewis, C. S., *Reflections on the Psalms* (G. Bles, 1958).

Magonet, Jonathan, *A Rabbi's Bible* (SCM Press, 1991).

Nygren, Anders, *Agape and Eros*, trans. Philip S. Watson (SPCK, 1953).

O'Neill, John C., *The Bible's Authority: A Portrait Gallery of Thinkers from Lessing to Bultmann* (T&T Clark, 1991).

Rosenthal, Franz, 'A Judaeo-Arabic Work under Sufic Influence', *Hebrew Union College Annual*, xv (1940), 433–84.

Rowland, Christopher, 'John 1.51, Jewish Apocalyptic and Targumic Tradition', *New Testament Studies*, 30 (1984), 498–507.

Saward, John, *Perfect Fools* (Oxford University Press, 1980)

Schechter, Solomon, ed., *Agadath Shir Hashirim, Edited from a Parma Manuscript. Annotated and Illustrated with Parallel Passages from Numerous MSS. and Early Prints, with a Postscript on the History of the Work* (Deighton Bell & Co., 1896).

Scholem, Gershom, *Jewish Gnosticism, Merkabah Mysticism and Talmudic Tradition* (The Jewish Theological Seminary of America, 1960).

——, *Kabbalah* (Quadrangle, 1974).

——, *Major Trends in Jewish Mysticism*, with a new Foreword by Robert Alter (Schocken Books, 1995).

——, *On the Kabbalah and its Symbolism* (Schocken, 1975).

——, *Origins of the Kabbalah*, ed. R. J. Zwi Werblowsky, trans. Allan Arkush (Princeton University Press, 1991).

Southern, Richard W., *Medieval Humanism* (Harper & Row, 1970).

Teresa of Ávila, *The Collected Works. Volume 2: The Way of Perfection, Meditations on the Song of Songs, The Interior Castle*, trans. Kieran Kavanagh OCD and Otilio Rodriguez OCD (Institute of Carmelite Studies, 1980).

Wenham, John, *The Enigma of Evil: Can We Believe in the Goodness of God?* (Inter-Varsity Press, 1985).

Williams, Rowan, ed., *The Making of Orthodoxy: Essays in Honour of Henry Chadwick* (Cambridge University Press, 1989).

Young, Frances, *The Art of Performance: Toward a Theology of Holy Scripture* (Darton, Longman and Todd, 1990).

Dictionaries and Commentaries

The Oxford Bible Commentary, ed. John Barton and John Muddiman (Oxford University Press, 2001).

Encyclopaedia Judaica, gen. ed. Michael Berenbaum (Thomson Gale, 2007).

A Dictionary of Biblical Interpretation, ed. R. J. Coggins and J. L. Houlden (SCM Press, 1990).

The Jewish Encyclopedia, ed. Isadore Singer (Funk and Wagnalls Company, 1907).

The World of the Aramaeans: Biblical Studies in Honour of Paul-Eugene Dion, Journal for the Study of the Old Testament, Supplement S., ed. Michele Daviau, John W. Wevers, Michael Weigl (Continuum International Publishing Group, 2001).

SLG PRESS PUBLICATIONS

FP1	*Prayer and the Life of Reconciliation*	Gilbert Shaw (1969)
FP2	*Aloneness not Loneliness*	Mother Mary Clare SLG (1969)
FP4	*Intercession*	Mother Mary Clare SLG (1969)
FP8	*Prayer: Extracts from the Teaching of Father Gilbert Shaw*	Gilbert Shaw (1973)
FP12	*Learning to Pray*	Mother Mary Clare SLG (1970, rev. 3/2025)
FP15	*Death, the Gateway to Life*	Gilbert Shaw (1971, 3/2024)
FP16	*The Victory of the Cross*	Dumitru Stăniloae (1970, 3/2023)
FP26	*The Message of Saint Seraphim*	Irina Gorainov (1974)
FP28	*Julian of Norwich: Four Studies to Commemorate the Sixth Centenary of the Revelations of Divine Love*	Sister Benedicta Ward SLG, Sister Eileen Mary SLG, Sister Mary Paul SLG, A. M. Allchin (1973, 3/2022)
FP43	*The Power of the Name: The Jesus Prayer in Orthodox Spirituality*	Kallistos Ware (1974)
FP46	*Prayer and Contemplation* and *Distractions are for Healing*	Robert Llewelyn (1975, rev. 4/2025)
FP48	*The Wisdom of the Desert Fathers*	trans. Sister Benedicta Ward SLG (1975)
FP50	*Letters of Saint Antony the Great*	trans. Derwas Chitty (1975, 2/2021)
FP54	*From Loneliness to Solitude*	Roland Walls (1976)
FP55	*Theology and Spirituality*	Andrew Louth (1976, rev. 1978, 3/2024)
FP61	*Kabir: The Way of Love and Paradox*	Sister Rosemary SLG (1977)
FP62	*Anselm of Canterbury: A Monastic Scholar*	Sister Benedicta Ward SLG (1973, 2/2024)
FP67	*Mary and the Mystery of the Incarnation: An Essay on the Mother of God in the Theology of Karl Barth*	Andrew Louth (1977, 2/2024)
FP68	*Trinity and Incarnation in Anglican Tradition*	A. M. Allchin (1977, rev. 2/2025)
FP70	*Facing Depression*	Gonville ffrench-Beytagh (1978, 2/2020)
FP71	*The Single Person*	Philip Welsh (1979)
FP72	*The Letters of Ammonas, Successor of St Antony*	trans. Derwas Chitty, introd. Sebastian Brock (1979, 2/2023)
FP74	*George Herbert, Priest and Poet*	Kenneth Mason (1980)
FP75	*A Study of Wisdom: Three Tracts by the Author of The Cloud of Unknowing*	trans. Clifton Wolters (1980)
FP81	*The Psalms: Prayer Book of the Bible*	Dietrich Bonhoeffer, trans. Sister Isabel SLG (1982, rev. 3/2025)
FP82	*Prayer & Holiness: The Icon of Man Renewed in God*	Dumitru Stăniloae (1982, rev. 2/2023)
FP85	*Walter Hilton: Eight Chapters on Perfection & Angels' Song*	trans. Rosemary Dorward (1983, rev. 3/2024)
FP88	*Creative Suffering*	Iulia de Beausobre (1989)
FP90	*Bringing Forth Christ: Five Feasts of the Child Jesus by St Bonaventure*	trans. Eric Doyle OFM (1984, 3/2024)
FP92	*Gentleness in John of the Cross*	Thomas Kane (1985, rev. 2/2025)
FP94	*Saint Gregory Nazianzen: Selected Poems*	trans. John McGuckin (1986, 2/2024)
FP95	*The World of the Desert Fathers: Stories and Sayings from the Anonymous Series of the Apophthegmata Patrum*	trans. Columba Stewart OSB (1986, 2/2020)
FP104	*Growing Old with God*	Timothy N. Rudd (1988, 2/2020)
FP106	*Julian Reconsidered*	Kenneth Leech, Sister Benedicta Ward SLG (1988/ rev. 2/2024)
FP108	*The Unicorn: Meditations on the Love of God*	Harry Galbraith Miller (1989)

FP109	*The Creativity of Diminishment*	Sister Anke (1990)
FP110	*Called to be Priests*	Hugh Wybrew (1989, updated 2/2024)
FP111	*A Kind of Watershed: An Anglican Lay View of Sacramental Confession*	
		Christine North (1990, updated 2/2022)
FP116	*Jesus, the Living Lord*	Bishop Michael Ramsey (1992)
FP120	*The Monastic Letters of Saint Athanasius the Great*	
		trans. and introd. Leslie Barnard (1994, 2/2023)
FP122	*The Hidden Joy*	Sister Jane SLG, ed. Dorothy Sutherland (1994)
FP124	*Prayer of the Heart: An Approach to Silent Prayer and Prayer in the Night*	
		Alexander Ryrie (1995, 3/2020)
FP126	*Evelyn Underhill, Anglican Mystic: Two Centenary Essays*	
		A. M. Allchin, Bishop Michael Ramsey (1977, rev. 4/2025)
FP127	*Apostolate and the Mirrors of Paradox*	
		Sydney Evans, ed. Andrew Linzey & Brian Horne (1996)
FP128	*The Wisdom of Saint Isaac the Syrian*	Sebastian Brock (1997)
FP129	*Saint Thérèse of Lisieux: Her Relevance for Today*	Sister Eileen Mary SLG (1997)
FP130	*Expectations: Five Addresses for Those Beginning Ministry*	Sister Edmée SLG (1997, 2/2024)
FP131	*Scenes from Animal Life: Fables for the Enneagram Types*	
		Waltraud Kirschke, trans. Sister Isabel SLG (1998)
FP132	*Praying the Word of God: The Use of Lectio Divina*	Charles Dumont OCSO (1999)
FP133	*Love Unknown: Meditations on the Death and Resurrection of Jesus*	
		John Barton (1999, 2/2024)
FP134	*The Hidden Way of Love: Jean-Pierre de Caussade's Spirituality of Abandonment*	
		Barry Conaway (1999, rev. 2/2025)
FP135	*Shepherd and Servant: The Spiritual Theology of Saint Dunstan*	Douglas Dales (2000)
FP137	*Pilgrimage of the Heart*	Sister Benedicta Ward SLG (2001)
FP138	*Mixed Life* Walter Hilton, trans. Rosemary Dorward (2001, enlarged rev. 3/2024)	
FP139	*In the Footsteps of the Lord: The Teaching of Abba Isaiah of Scetis*	
		John Chryssavgis, Luke Penkett (2001, 2/2023)
FP140	*A Great Joy: Reflections on the Meaning of Christmas*	Kenneth Mason (2001)
FP141	*Bede and the Psalter*	Sister Benedicta Ward SLG (2002, 2/2024)
FP142	*Abhishiktananda: A Memoir of Dom Henri Le Saux* Murray Rogers, David Barton (2003)	
FP143	*Friendship in God: The Encounter of Evelyn Underhill & Sorella Maria of Campello*	
		A. M. Allchin (2003, rev. 2/2025)
FP144	*Christian Imagination in Poetry and Polity: Some Anglican Voices from Temple to Herbert*	
		Bishop Rowan Williams (2004)
FP145	*The Reflections of Abba Zosimas: Monk of the Palestinian Desert*	
		trans. and introd. John Chryssavgis (2005, 3/2022)
FP146	*The Gift of Theology: The Trinitarian Vision of Ann Griffiths and Elizabeth of Dijon*	
		A. M. Allchin (2005)
FP147	*Sacrifice and Spirit*	Bishop Michael Ramsey (2005)
FP148	*Saint John Cassian on Prayer*	trans. A. M. Casiday (2006, 2/2024)
FP149	*Hymns of Saint Ephrem the Syrian*	trans. Mary Hansbury (2006, 2/2024)
FP150	*Suffering: Why All this Suffering? What Do I Do about It?*	
		Reinhard Körner OCD, trans. Sister Avis Mary SLG (2006)
FP151	*A True Easter: The Synod of Whitby 664 AD* Sister Benedicta Ward SLG (2007, 2/2023)	
FP152	*Prayer as Self-Offering*	Alexander Ryrie (2007)
FP153	*From Perfection to the Elixir: How George Herbert Fashioned a Famous Poem*	
		Benedick de la Mare (2008, 2/2024)
FP154	*The Jesus Prayer: Gospel Soundings*	Sister Pauline Margaret CHN (2008)

FP155	Loving God Whatever: Through the Year with Sister Jane	Sister Jane SLG (2006)
FP156	Prayer and Meditation for a Sleepless Night	Sisters of the Love of God (1993, 3/2024)
FP157	Being There: Caring for the Bereaved	John Porter (2009)
FP158	Learn to Be at Peace: The Practice of Stillness	Andrew Norman (2010)
FP159	From Holy Week to Easter	George Pattison (2010)
FP160	Strength in Weakness: The Scandal of the Cross	John W. Rogerson (2010)
FP161	Augustine Baker: Frontiers of the Spirit	Victor de Waal (2010, rev. 2/2025)
FP162	Out of the Depths	Gonville ffrench-Beytagh; epilogue Wendy Robinson (1990, 2/2010)
FP163	God and Darkness: A Carmelite Perspective	Gemma Hinricher OCD, trans. Sister Avis Mary SLG (2010)
FP164	The Gift of Joy	Curtis Almquist SSJE (2011)
FP165	'I Have Called You Friends': Suggestions for the Spiritual Life Based on the Farewell Discourses of Jesus	Reinhard Körner OCD (2012)
FP166	Leisure	Mother Mary Clare SLG (2012)
FP167	Carmelite Ascent: An Introduction to Saint Teresa and Saint John of the Cross	Mother Mary Clare SLG (1973, rev. 2/2012)
FP168	Ann Griffiths and Her Writings	Llewellyn Cumings (2012)
FP169	The Our Father	Sister Benedicta Ward SLG (2012)
FP171	The Spiritual Wisdom of the Syriac Book of Steps	Robert A. Kitchen (2013)
FP172	The Prayer of Silence	Alexander Ryrie (2012)
FP173	On Tour in Byzantium: Excerpts from The Spiritual Meadow of John Moschus	Ralph Martin SSM (2013)
FP174	Monastic Life	Bonnie Thurston (2016)
FP175	Shall All Be Well? Reflections for Holy Week	Graham Ward (2015)
FP176	Solitude and Communion: Papers on the Hermit Life	ed. A. M. Allchin (2015)
FP177	The Prayers of Jacob of Serugh	ed. Mary Hansbury (2015)
FP178	The Monastic Hours of Prayer	Sister Benedicta Ward SLG (2016)
FP179	The Desert of the Heart: Daily Readings with the Desert Fathers	trans. Sister Benedicta Ward SLG (2016)
FP180	In Company with Christ: Lent, Palm Sunday, Good Friday & Easter to Pentecost	Sister Benedicta Ward SLG (2016)
FP181	Lazarus: Come Out! Reflections on John 11	Bonnie Thurston (2017)
FP182	Unknowing & Astonishment: Meditations on Faith for the Long Haul	Christopher Scott (2018)
FP183	Pondering, Praying, Preaching: Romans 8	Bonnie Thurston (2019, 2/2021)
FP184	Shem'on the Graceful: Discourse on the Solitary Life	trans. and introd. Mary Hansbury (2020)
FP185	God Under My Roof: Celtic Songs and Blessings	Esther de Waal (2020)
FP186	Journeying with the Jesus Prayer	James F. Wellington (2020)
FP187	Poet of the Word: Re-reading Scripture with Ephraem the Syrian	Aelred Partridge OC (2020)
FP188	Identity and Ritual	Alan Griffiths (2021)
FP189	River of the Spirit: The Spirituality of Simon Barrington-Ward	Andy Lord (2021)
FP190	Prayer and the Struggle against Evil	John Barton, Daniel Lloyd, James Ramsay, Alexander Ryrie (2021)
FP191	Dante's Spiritual Journey: A Reading of the Divine Comedy	Tony Dickinson (2021)
FP192	Jesus the Undistorted Image of God	John Townroe (2022)
FP193	Our Deepest Desire: Prayer, Fasting & Almsgiving in the Writings of	

	Saint Augustine of Hippo	Sister Susan SLG (2022)
FP194	Lent with George Herbert	Tony Dickinson (2022)
FP195	Four Ways to the Cross	Tony Dickinson (2022)
FP196	Anselm of Canterbury, Teacher of Prayer	Sister Benedicta Ward SLG (2022)
FP197	With One Heart and Mind: Prayers out of Stillness	Anthony Kemp (2023)
FP198	Sayings of the Urban Fathers & Mothers	James Ashdown (2023)
FP199	Doors	Sister Raphael SLG (2023)
FP200	Monastic Vocation SISTERS OF THE LOVE OF GOD, Bishop Rowan Williams (2021)	
FP201	An Ecology of the Heart: Faith Through the Climate Crisis	Duncan Forbes (2023)
FP202	'In the image of the Image': Gregory of Nyssa's Opposition to Slavery	
		Adam Couchman (2023)
FP203	Gregory of Nyssa and the Sins of Asia Minor	Jonathan Farrugia (2023)
FP204	Discovery	Arthur Bell (2023)
FP205	Living Healing: the Spirituality of Leanne Payne	Andy Lord (2023)
FP206	Still Listening: Sowing the Seeds of the Jesus Prayer	Bruce Batstone CJN (2023)
FP207	Julian of Norwich: Four Essays to Commemorate 650 Years of the	
	Revelations of Divine Love Bishop Graham Usher, Father Colin CSWG,	
	Sister Elizabeth Ruth Obbard OC, Mother Hilary Crupi OJN (2023)	
FP208	TIME	Dumitru Stăniloae, Kallistos Ware (2023)
FP209	Pearls of Life: A Lifebelt for the Spirit	Tony Dickinson (2024)
FP210	The Way and the Truth and the Life: An Exploration by a Follower of the Way	
		James Ramsay (2024)
FP211	Cosmos, Crisis & Christ: Essays of Wendy Robinson	Wendy Robinson (2024)
FP212	Towards a Theology of Psychotherapy: The Spirituality of Wendy Robinson	
		Andrew Louth (2024)
FP213	Immersed in God and the World: Living Priestly Ministry	Andy Lord (2024)
FP214	The Road to Emmaus: A Sculptor's Journey through Time	Rodney Munday (2024)
FP215	Prayer Too Deep for Words	Sister Edmée SLG (2024)
FP216	The Prayers of St Isaac of Nineveh	Sebastian Brock (2024)
FP217	Two Medieval English Saints: Cuthbert and Alban	Sister Benedicta Ward SLG (2024)
FP218	Encountering the Depths	Mother Mary Clare SLG (1981, rev. 3/2024)
FP219	Conflict and Concord Sister Susan SLG, Bishop Humphrey Southern,	
	Bronwen Neil, Sister Rosemary SLG, Sister Clare-Louise SLG (2024)	
FP220	Divine Love in the Song of Songs	Sister Edmée SLG (2024)
FP221	Zeal for the Faith: An Introduction to Christian-Muslim Dialogue Tony Dickinson (2024)	
FP222	Bernard & Abelard	Sister Edmée SLG (2024)
FP223	Eliot's Transitions: T. S. Eliot's Search for Identity and the Society	
	of the Sacred Mission at Kelham Hall	Vincent Strudwick (2024)
FP224	Landscape, Soul and Spirit: Ecology, Prayer and Robert Macfarlane	Andy Lord (2025)
FP225	Our Home is in God	John Townroe (2025)
FP226	Signs of the Times: A Brief Survey of the Bible's Apocalyptic Writings Tony Dickinson (2025)	
FP227	And We Shall be Changed: Christian Reflections on Death and Dying James Ramsay (2025)	
FP228	Journeys into the Bible	Sister Edmée SLG (2025)
FP226	Directions	Sister Edmée SLG (2025)

www.slgpress.co.uk

Contemplative Poetry series

CP1	*Amado Nervo: Poems of Faith and Doubt*	trans. John Gallas (2021)
CP2	*Anglo-Saxon Poets: The High Roof of Heaven*	trans. John Gallas (2021)
CP3	*Middle English Poets: Where Grace Grows Ever Green*	ed. John Gallas (2021)
CP4	*The Voice inside Our Home: Selected Poems*	Edward Clarke (2022)
CP5	*Women & God: Drops in the Sea of Time*	trans. and ed. John Gallas (2022)
CP6	*Gabrielle de Coignard & Vittoria Colonna: Fly Not Too High*	trans. John Gallas (2022)
CP7	*Chancing on Sanctity: Selected Poems*	James Ramsay (2022)
CP8	*Gabriela Mistral: This Far Place*	trans. John Gallas (2023)
CP9	*Henry Vaughan & George Herbert: Divine Themes and Celestial Praise*	ed. Edward Clarke (2023)
CP10	*Love Will Come with Fire: Anthology*	Sisters of the Love of God (2023)
CP11	*Touchpapers: Anthology*	coll. and trans. John Gallas (2023)
CP12	*Seasons of my Soul: Selected Poems*	Clare McKerron (2023)
CP13	*Reinhard Sorge: Take Flight to God*	trans. John Gallas (2024)
CP14	*Embertide: Encountering Saint Frideswide*	Romola Parish (2024)
CP15	*Thomas Campion: Made All of Light*	ed. and introd. Julia Craig-McFeely (2024)
CP16	*When God Hides: Selected Poems*	Joseph Evans (2025)

Vestry Guides

VG1	*The Visiting Minister: How to Welcome Visiting Clergy to Your Church*	Paul Monk (2021)
VG2	*Help! No Minister! or Please Take the Service*	Paul Monk (2022)
VG3	*The Liturgy of the Eucharist: An Introductory Guide*	Paul Monk (2024)

www.slgpress.co.uk

The Sisters of the Love of God is an Anglican community of women religious living a contemplative monastic life.

To learn more about the Community and the Convent of the Incarnation at Fairacres, Oxford, see our website www.slg.org.uk.

As well as supporting those seeking to follow a vocation to the monastic life, the Community has a number of forms of association for those who feel drawn to share in the Sisters' life of prayer: Fellowship of the Love of God, Companions, Priests Associate or Oblate Sisters.

For more information email sisters@slg.org.uk or write to The Reverend Mother, Convent of the Incarnation, Parker Street, Oxford, OX4 1TB, UK.